The Complete Miniature Quilt Book

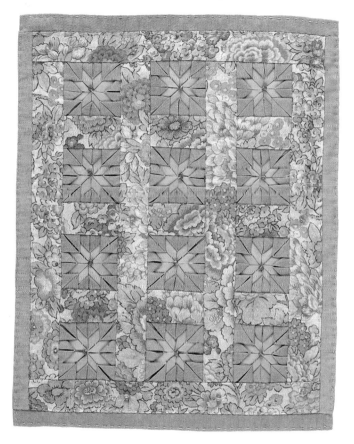

The Complete Miniature Quilt Book

Over 24 Projects for Quilters and Doll's House Enthusiasts

Dinah Travis

krause publications

since 1952

700 E. State Street • Iola, WI 54990-0001

Text and designs © Dinah Travis 1998

The moral right of the author has been asserted.

Photographs and color line illustrations
© B. T. Batford 1998

ʘ98 Gen Fund 20.⁰⁰
ISBN 0-87341-595-7

CIP 98 - 80608

Second publication in the United States by Krause
Publications **krause publications**
700 E. State Street • Iola, WI 54990-0001

Please call or write for free catalog of publications.

Orders: 800 258-0929

Editorial comment: 715 445-2214

This book was first published, designed and produced
by: B.T. Batsford Ltd,

583 Fulham Road, London SW6 5BY

Printed in China

Photography by Michael Wicks

Color line illustrations by Penny Brown

Designed by DWN Ltd., London

Acknowledgements

I would like to express my thanks to my colleague
Pat Salt for her support and willingness to work
with me investigating more and more ideas for
quiltmaking and for making the paper and the
embellished quilts; Gilbert Travis for his support in
reading the text and for making the doll's house for
displaying my quilts; Peter Alden of Doll's House
Holidays with whom Gilbert made the house; Peter
Fear for his enthusiasm for designing and making
the brass bed; Mary Webb who passed on her
enthusiasm and knowledge of making miniatures
for the doll's house (the pine bed is based on one
made with her); Joan Fogg for giving me the
appliqué quilt; the students of Bromley Adult
Education College for learning about my ideas and
making them work; Lyn Thompson from Doll's
House Parade for the loan of furniture for the doll's
house photographs and finally the team at Batsford
for their support in producing the book.

CONTENTS

INTRODUCTION   7

CHAPTER 1
MATERIALS AND BASIC TECHNIQUES 9
Planning and Designing the Quilt   10
Materials and Tools   16
Basic Quiltmaking Techniques   21

CHAPTER 2
THE QUILTS   27
Hexagon Quilt   28
Painted Quilt   32
Log Cabin Quilt   34
Block Quilt   38
Suffolk Puff Quilt   42
Roman Stripes Quilt   44
Hawaiian Quilt   47
Kantha Quilt   50
Wholecloth Quilt   52
Somerset Star Quilt   54
Crazy Quilt   57
Printed Quilt   60
Appliqué Quilt   65
Felt Quilt   66
Mola Quilt   68
Quilt of Squares   70

Tucked Quilt   73
Cathedral Window Quilt   76
Knotted Quilt   78
Paper Quilt   80
Frayed Quilt   82
Embellished Quilt   84
Stencilled Quilt   86
Sashiko Quilt   89

CHAPTER 3
THE QUILT ON SHOW   93
Double Brass Bed   94
Cradle   97
Cot   98
Single Pine Bed   100
Mattress and Pillows   102
Blankets and Bed Linen   103
Quilt Stand   104
The Doll's House   106
Care of the Quilts   109

FURTHER READING   110

INDEX   112

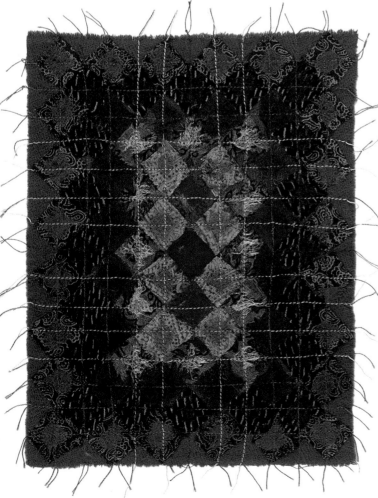

Introduction

A miniature is a small-scale representation of a full-size object. It is difficult to differentiate between a true miniature and simply a small full-size object, but the eye does this for us in interpreting the images we see.

The quilts in this book are planned and made to $\frac{1}{12}$th the normal size; that is a scale of 1 in to represent 1 ft. The $\frac{1}{12}$th scale is that most commonly used by doll's house enthusiasts; quilts made to this size also look very attractive as pictures or as small, precious wall hangings. However, as the materials and techniques suggested are those generally used in full-size quiltmaking, in some cases it is impossible to obtain a true representation of the $\frac{1}{12}$th scale. The scale demands the use of the finest fabrics and threads and a technique that is suitable for the quilt being made. For instance, a technique that is bulky will not allow the quilt to bend or drape. If this is a requirement, then it would be best to choose a technique that uses the least number of layers of fabric in the construction. I have therefore not only looked at traditional techniques but in some cases have made suggestions on how to adapt these techniques to give the feel of the small scale. An effective use of color or tone can also create a sense of the miniature.

A few of the quilts described in this book explore the use of modern materials. For most quilts, however, I have described the traditional method and then suggested other ways of creating the true miniature scale. In some cases I have also given an easier technique for those with limited time.

It does not follow that because a quilt is small it will be quick to make: a quilt of traditional hexagons will take just as long to make as a larger quilt with the same number of pieces. The advantage of the miniature is that, unlike a full size quilt, it is easily portable, making it possible to work whenever and wherever the opportunity arises (I made the cathedral window quilt illustrated on page 77 on a camping holiday).

Note that when square miniature quilts are viewed flat they are often not perceived as miniatures at all but simply as cushion covers. My advice therefore is that miniature quilts should be made in a rectangular format when they are to be viewed flat, such as in a wall hanging, and only made square when they are to be displayed on a bed or draped elsewhere.

Any of the quilts in this book can be enlarged to make a full-size quilt – simply scale them up. For example, a 6 x 8 in quilt would make a 72 x 96 in single bed quilt.

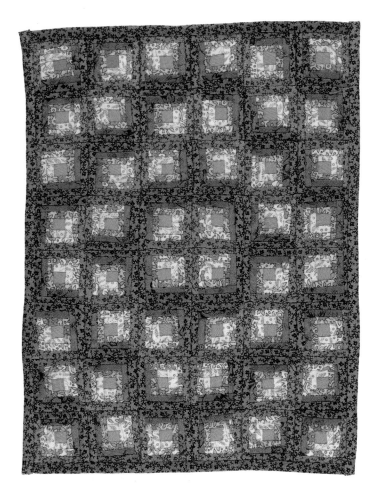

Chapter 1
Materials and Basic Techniques

To embark on planning and making a miniature quilt you will first need to collect a selection of drawing tools, equipment and materials for drawing out the plan, for developing the design, for preparing templates and for creating the quilt. All these materials and tools will influence the result. The use of the best and finest quality fabrics together with the smallest tools in a clean environment will go a long way to helping you produce a precious quilt worthy of all your efforts.

First, put your ideas down on paper. Starting to sew without planning means that all sorts of things can go wrong. Much effort can be saved sorting out the size or colour scheme in the early stages of designing. Having planned the layout and the techniques, the work of making the quilt can now move forward with only minor problems.

There are many traditional patchwork and quilting techniques from which to select. The basic ones are described. The more unusual ones are included where relevant in instructions for making the individual quilts. These include the exciting methods of feltmaking, printing, stenciling and embellishing a surface. Experiment with both traditional and less familiar techniques to create a unique piece.

However or whatever choices you make, the best advice is to keep each stage as simple as possible.

PLANNING AND DESIGNING THE QUILT

DRAWING TOOLS

You will need:

- A ruler clearly marked with a small scale. Metal rulers are ideal as they rest flat on the paper, making it easier to draw lines in exactly the right place (a small discrepancy of measurement is easily made with a bevelled ruler by angling the pencil too acutely).

- A set square or a protractor to ensure that your drawings are square. An angle minutely misdrawn shows up particularly in small items.

- A compass to draw any size of circle required and to bisect angles.

- A hard (H) pencil to draw accurate lines and a soft (B) pencil for making quick sketches.

- Paints or pens for colored designs. Watercolor pencils are also useful for an immediate impression of an idea.

- A brush to use wet with the watercolor pencils so that the colors of a drawing swim and work like watercolor paints.

- Sharp scissors kept specifically for paper (paper blunts scissors, making them unusable for fabric).

- Cartridge paper for color design work and ¼ in squared paper for scaled drawings.

- Thin card or plastic for making templates.

RECORDING THE FIRST IDEAS

First, find a picture you like and which suggests an idea to you, no matter how remote or obscure. This could be a favourite picture, a photograph or an illustration from a magazine. From this picture take suggestions for color and shapes by pinning a selection of small pieces of fabric to a piece of paper. Next, make a colored sketch on squared paper with crayons, paints or pens, or a combination of any of these. Now think about translating the shapes in a way more closely related to traditional patchwork pieces: flowers or fruit could be represented by circles of various sizes, buildings by squares and oblongs, and the sails of boats by triangles. By experimenting in this way you will soon come across an idea that can successfully be translated into quilt technique.

MAKING A PLAN FOR THE QUILT

For your first miniature quilt the easiest shapes to start with are squares. First decide on the size of the quilt and draw its outline. (Fig. 1 shows the outline sizes of various quilts in $\frac{1}{12}$th scale.) Next, divide the outline shape into however many squares you think appropriate. Remember that the smaller the dimension of the squares, the more it will help to create the feel of the miniature in the finished quilt. You now have a basic plan for your quilt.

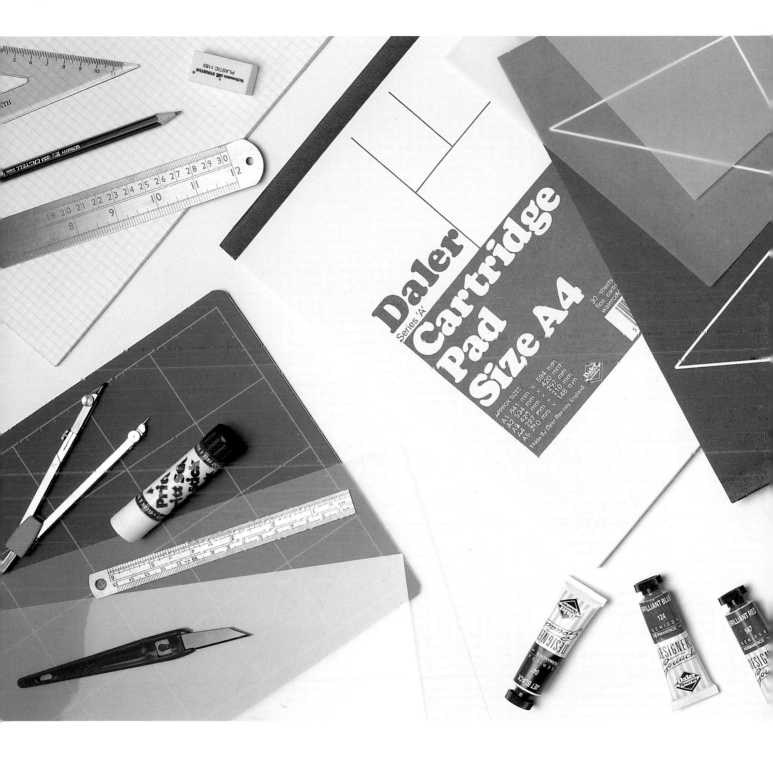

Fig. 1a–f
Plan of quilt sizes

Fig. 1a
Cradle quilt: 38 x 51 mm (1½ x 2 in)

Fig. 1b
Cot quilt: 50 x 7.5 cm (2 x 3 in)

Fig. 1c
Single bed quilt: 15 x 15 cm
(6 x 6 in) without tuck-in

Fig. 1d
Single bed quilt: 15 x 20 cm
(6 x 8 in) with tuck-in

Fig 1e
Double bed quilt: 20 x 15 cm
(8 x 6 in) without tuck-in

Fig. 1f
Double bed quilt: 20 x 20 cm
(8 x 8 in) with tuck-in

DESIGNING THE QUILT

Make several copies of your plan – a photocopier is useful for this. Colour these plans in different ways, using your first colour ideas as a guide. Experiment – by colouring one plan with alternate dark and light squares, another with colours shading from dark to light across the design, and another grouping different colours together. Continue in this way to create a wealth of designs for a quilt of squares, then choose the best.

For more complex designs, draw the plan in the same way, but introduce repeated blocks, sashing, borders or any other desireable details. With some geometric shapes it may be easier to use a ready-made metal template to help draw out the basic plan. These can be purchased from specialist patchwork and quilting suppliers. Otherwise, draw out one shape to size accurately and trace it onto plastic. Cut out the plastic shape to make a firm template that will stand up to repeated use (a card template soon deteriorates under constant battering from a pencil).

If you are making a patchwork quilt in which the patches are sewn over papers, copy the design onto thick paper such as cartridge paper (a photocopy shop should be able to copy it onto thin card to save having to draw the plan out again). You can then cut up this copy to create the papers.

For block patchwork, the design can be drawn directly from the plan onto the fabric that has been chosen as a base. Fix the plan to a table or board with masking tape, then secure the fabric over it with more tape. Trace the plan or part of the plan, depending on what is required, onto the fabric ready for sewing.

Details of the basic sewing techniques are described on pages 21–25, followed by the instructions for making the individual quilts in Chapter 2.

ornamental cabbages

Miniature Suffolk Puff Quilt

finished size 6" x 8"

1¼" template makes 1" puff

Puff actual size

MATERIALS AND TOOLS

All the materials and tools used in making a miniature quilt will influence the result. The use of the finest quality fabrics, and the smallest tools in a clean environment will go a long way towards helping you sew neatly in a miniaturist's scale to produce a precious quilt.

There are many fabrics, interlinings and threads readily available, produced for all sorts of uses, so investigate what's on offer and choose the most appropriate for the job in hand.

FABRICS

The miniature quilt, like a full-size traditional quilt, needs a top, an interlining and a backing fabric. In traditional full-size quilts the top was a cotton fabric, such as a sateen for plain quilts, or cotton prints sewn into patterns for patchwork and appliqué quilts. Woolen fabrics were also used in some quilts. The interlining consisted of cotton wadding, carded wool or an old blanket. The backing was similar to the top fabric.

The top and backing fabrics of miniature quilts need to be woven from fine threads, making them as light in weight as possible so that they will hang in fine drapes in the same way as a full-size quilt. Both cotton lawn and habutai silk have this quality and are readily available from the fabric departments of large stores.

Recycling cotton fabric from an old garment such as a nightie can supply you with beautifully soft, easily manageable fabric. The disadvantage of this method is that salvaged white material is often

fairly transparent. Plain, 'recycled' fabrics are also often ideal as a base for blocks of patchwork because they are lightweight and transparent enough to trace a pencil drawing.

The color and size of the print should be different from those used on a full-size quilt. Color and print size help to create a feeling of scale, so even when it is not possible to actually sew patchwork to the correct scale, the print or a selected part of the print will help to suggest the illusion of small size. The intensity of the color of a fabric will also suggest a feel for size: the brighter the print, the more pronounced it will appear, making it seem larger. You should therefore subdue your ideas of colour slightly from those used on a full-size quilt. Also consider the tone of the colors when choosing a scheme: closer toned colors will be gentle to the eye and more readily suit a given situation. You will find that the balance of colors and tone in a miniature are completely different to those of a full-size quilt. This is what makes it difficult for the traditional quilter to adapt to making what to them might seem a simple practical task. Remember that the obvious is not always the answer.

INTERLININGS

Like the outer fabric, the interlining of the quilt sandwich needs to be flexible and fine. Traditional cotton wadding is quite thin and is both soft enough and flat enough to represent the thickness of a full-size quilt in miniature. It has a paper-like backing which can be removed to reduce the thickness. Silk wadding imported from China is very fine and light in weight, and can be divided or pulled apart to make it thinner. Some of the man-made waddings are easily pulled into two thin layers, and can also be pressed under a damp cloth with a cool iron to compress them even more. However, when compressed the synthetic waddings are not as flexible as the cotton or silk waddings, and are therefore more suitable for use in a wall hanging or an eiderdown-type quilt. A single layer of fabric can also act as wadding, much as the old blanket did in traditional full-size quilts. Remember that the fabric needs to be flexible and soft – fine woven wool, flannel or old sheeting are all ideal.

THREADS

I prefer to use a fine sewing thread – usually a number 50 thread in 100 per cent cotton. Many manufacturers do not label their threads for thickness, so you will have to experiment with those you already have to decide which are most suitable. In some instances you will find that you have to tug the thread more than usual; you may find that a fine, man-made thread is better in such cases. A fine, soft tacking thread is important as these threads easily get in the way and need to be removed quickly when you are placing the needle precisely for a stitch. Color is also important; a good match of thread to fabric will help to hide what would otherwise seem an over-large stitch for the miniature scale you are working in. The many colors of the stranded embroidery cotton threads are useful for any surface stitching, but not where strength is needed.

When using a sewing machine I also choose as fine a thread as possible. The double thread of a machine stitch can often be clumsy and intrusive.

PINS

I use fine, long pins (such as the Japanese ones that are bought in a packet just like needles) and also short pins called lilles, which are only ½ in long.

long. The lilles are delicate and are suitable for holding any part of a miniature quilt sandwich. I use a pin cushion for the small pins as I find it easier to take hold of one from a cushion rather than fumbling around in a box. Lace pins or brass pins are also suitable.

NEEDLES

Choose as fine a needle as you are happy handling – the finer the needle the easier it is to make small stitches. I use 'number 10 quilting between' needles but as these are short you may be more comfortable with ordinary 'between' needles which are slightly longer. Fine chenille needles are also popular as they have a long eye and are therefore easier to thread.

I find that in gripping longer needles firmly I often bend them, making them difficult to use. If you are like me, keep an ample supply of needles and change any as soon as they start to bend. I find it easiest to keep needles in their original packages as it is difficult to determine their sizes if they are kept in a pin cushion.

SCISSORS

I use my normal sewing scissors for cutting out any fabrics, but when working on a small quilt I have a small pair with sharp points. This pair enables me to get very close to the fabric surface so that I can cut away thread ends and any small, unwanted pieces of fabric. Sharpen your scissors regularly: blunt scissors can easily cause a miscut which in turn may spoil the critical edge of a piece of fabric.

THIMBLES

It is not fashionable to use a thimble but they do help to regulate the size of stitching and to keep the work neat, as well as protecting your finger. The thimble needs to fit snugly on the middle finger to allow you to push the needle through the fabric once it has been placed there by the thumb and first finger. I like thimbles with a ridge round the head as this stops the needle slipping.

TEMPLATES

Small templates can be purchased from specialist suppliers, but it is best to make your own. Draw the shapes onto thin card or plastic and cut them out accurately using a craft knife and metal rule on a cutting board. Making them yourself means that they are exactly the right size for your needs.

PIN BOARD

For convenience and ease of handling, and to reduce the risk of losing the small pieces, I use a small pin board. I place the patches on this in the form of the quilt, removing them as it progresses.

UNUSUAL MATERIALS

Unusual materials required for certain quilts are discussed in the text where relevant.

WORKPLACE

The space needed for making a miniature is not large, but you do need good light and a clean surface on which to work. Light can be supplied by working under a window during the day and at night with a good, angled light shining directly onto your work but away from your eyes. Work at a table as small items are easily lost if you sit with your sewing on your knee. A container for your tools is also very useful.

BASIC QUILTMAKING TECHNIQUES

PATCHWORK

The best general advice for making miniature quilts is to keep the construction technique as simple as possible. The most common patchwork and quilting techniques are covered here, but more specialized techniques are described in the instructions for the individual quilts.

Sewing pieces together over papers

This method of joining pieces together may be used for any tessellating shapes with straight sides. Cut out the shapes required in thick paper, such as cartridge paper. Use this template to cut out the fabric, but allow approximately ⅛ in as a border around the paper shapes. Place the paper shape on the wrong side of the fabric shape and pin the centre (see Fig. 2a). Turn the extra fabric over the edge of the paper shape, tacking in place as you proceed (see Figs. 2b and 2c). Join two patches together by placing them face to face and oversewing by hand along one side (see Fig 2d). As the patching progresses, some shapes may need to be folded so that they can more easily be joined. Continue to join the patches in this way until the patchwork design is complete. Make quite sure that all fastenings on and off are securely held.

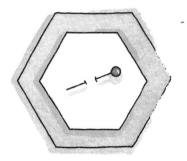

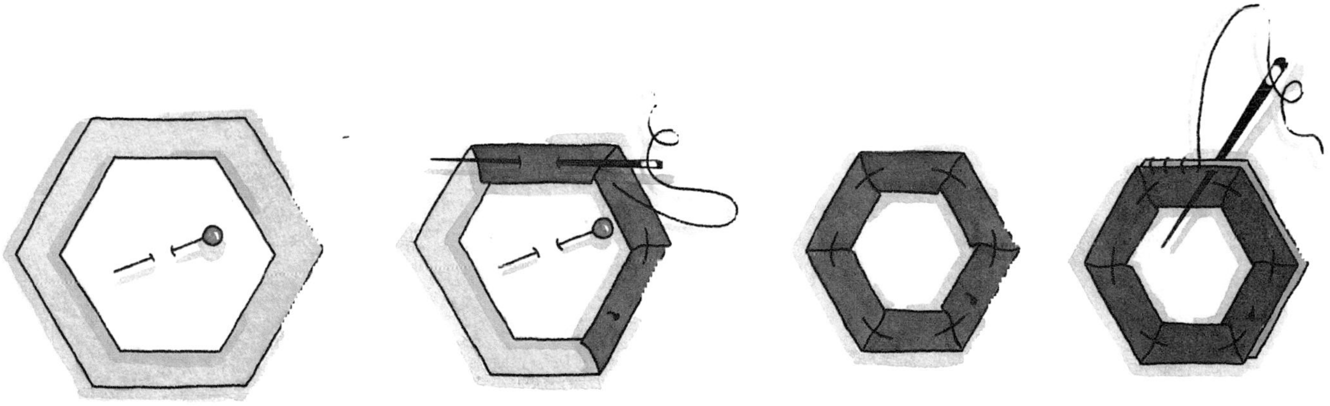

Fig. 2a

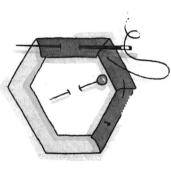

Fig. 2b

Fig. 2c

Fig. 2d

Fig. 2a–d
Sewing over papers

Sewing pieces together without papers

Cut out the shapes in fabric, allowing a ⅛ in seam allowance. Mark the seam allowance on the back of the shapes. Join two patches together by placing them face to face, pinning across the seam and sewing together along the marked line. Use a simple running stitch with an occasional back stitch or a small machine stitch. Sew more pieces together in the same way, organizing the order of sewing so that, if possible, you avoid sewing round corners – if you do not, you will find that it is difficult to make the patchwork lie flat.

Sewing pieces onto a backing fabric

For this method the layout of the quilt should be divided into manageable units. Cut a piece of plain white backing fabric the size of a unit, adding a small seam allowance all round. Mark the design of the piecing onto the back of this fabric. Cut pieces of fabric for the design, adding extra all round to allow for turnings. Decide on the order of piecing the design so that you will be able to sew one shape to another without having to sew round a corner (this may take a little practice). Place the first piece face up on the front of the backing fabric to correspond with its place in the design. Place the second piece face to face on the first piece and pin in position. Sew the seam through all three layers, from the marked side, using a small running stitch. Fasten on and off securely. Turn the second piece over into place. Continue adding pieces in this way in order to complete the design unit. The units can then be sewn together.

APPLIQUÉ

There are many ways of applying fabric shapes to a backing fabric, the choice depending on the quality of the fabric. A fine fabric shape to be applied may be cut out with a bare ⅛ in seam allowance. It is pinned in place, tacked and then sewn onto the backing fabric. A small, neat hemming stitch is used and the edge is turned under as you proceed round the shape (Fig. 3a).

In this method the stitching can be made virtually invisible by using a matching sewing thread.

If a firmer fabric is used it may be cut out exactly to shape and then placed, pinned and tacked onto the backing fabric. The shape can then be sewn down using a buttonhole (blanket) stitch

for a definite outline (Fig. 3c) or a herringbone stitch for a flexible flowing outline round the edge of the shape (Fig. 3b). The popular zigzag machine stitch is heavy and stiff, and not at all practical for miniature appliqué work.

A clean, clear shape may be applied using a fusible webbing. Draw the shape onto the paper side of the fusible webbing and iron this onto the reverse side of the fabric, following the manufacturer's instructions. Cut out the shape. Peel off the paper backing and iron the shape onto the backing fabric using a damp cloth. This method is suitable for small, intricate shapes.

Another way of dealing with detailed shapes is to cut them out, place a minute amount of paste on the reverse side and then stick them in position on the backing fabric. Next, cover them over with a sheer fabric the same size as the quilt top; this will hold many small, intricate pieces in place, quilting around each piece holding it secure. The paste will wash out once the quilt has been laundered.

Fig. 3a
Hemming stitch

Fig. 3b
Herringbone stitch

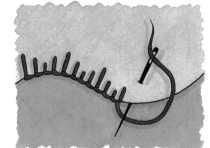

Fig. 3c
Buttonhole (blanket) stitch

KNOTTING

Using a strong thread, make a stitch through all the layers of the quilt sandwich. Next, make another stitch in the same spot. Pull both ends of the thread and tie a reef knot (see Fig. 4).

Fig. 5a

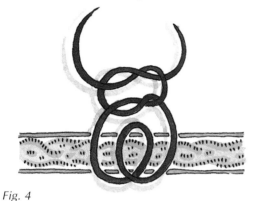

Fig. 4
Reef knot, used for tying the layers of a quilt together

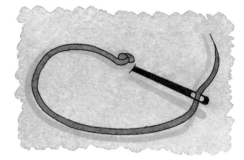

Fig. 5b

Traditionally the ends of the threads are left fairly long and hanging free. However, they may be hidden within the quilt sandwich if you do not like the look of them. This method was used for the French knot in the hexagon quilt on page 28 (Fig. 5a–c).

QUILTING

Choose your quilting thread according to the effect required. First, make a knot at the end of the thread. Put your needle into the quilt sandwich close to where you want to quilt and bring it out where you want to start, pulling the knot through so that it embeds in the interlining. Start quilting by using a running stitch which goes through all the layers of the sandwich. Make one or more stitches at a time or stab stitch from top to back and back to top. To finish, make a back stitch and run the thread into the layers of the sandwich or make a knot in the thread close to the top and pull it into the layers. The start and finish are invisible.

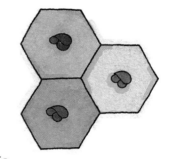

Fig. 5c

QUILT EDGES

A traditional edge often seen on old quilts is the butted edge. The top of the quilt and the wadding are trimmed to match, and the seam allowances are turned over together and tacked. The backing is then turned in to match the front. The top and backing are tacked and sewn together by slip stitching and then hemming in place, or a quilting stitch is run close to the folded edge. Before the two folded edges are tacked and sewn together a variety of insertions can be made into the seams, such as prairie points, piping, rickrack, pleats and frills.

Another turned edge is a self-bound edge, where the top of the quilt is turned over onto the back or the back of the quilt is turned over onto the top and hemmed in place.

A simple edge is formed by trimming all the layers of the quilt to match and then applying a straight binding separately onto all four sides of the quilt. Tack the matching edges together and attach a binding on two opposite sides first and then on the other two sides, finishing the corners off square. Only mitre corners if necessary to fit in with the design of the quilt. The bindings can be cut on the straight of the grain of the fabric unless the edge of the quilt is curved.

The simplest edge is formed by sewing the layers of the quilt together with a quilting stitch at a measured distance from the sides, leaving all the edges free. Different colored layers cut at various levels make a very attractive shimmer of color along this edge.

BASIC QUILT CONSTRUCTION

A traditional quilt is made from a sandwich of layers of fabric quilted together. It is made up from a top, which might be pieced, appliquéd or plain, an interlining and a back.

The back and the interlining should be slightly larger than the top. To make the quilt sandwich, lay the back of the quilt face down and place the interlining and the quilt top centrally on it. Pin these together, placing the pins in the same direction to allow for any movement of the fabrics. Tack across the sandwich in lines in one direction and then add lines at right angles to these. Unlike the method for full-size quilts, where the edge is finished last, prepare and tack the edge at this stage before finishing in the appropriate way for the technique used. Quilt or knot and then sew the edge to complete the quilt.

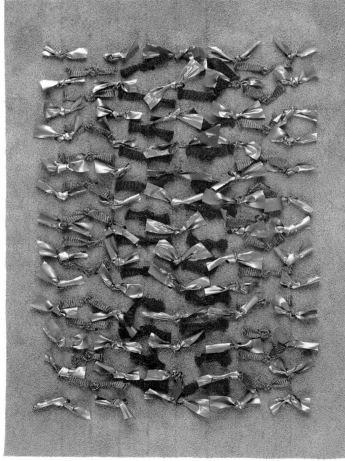

Chapter 2
The Quilts

There are quilts here, both easy and more complex, for anybody to make. Those who like a traditional British style will find the well-known technique of piecing hexagons over papers in the hexagon quilt, and the wholecloth quilt is a plain-quilted Welsh quilt. The crazy quilt evokes a romantic Victorian-era feeling and the log cabin quilt is for those with a pioneering spirit. For those who wish to be thrifty, the quilt of squares will use up scraps of fabric and the paper and knotted quilts recycle newsprint and plastic. The design of the Hawaiian quilt revives memories of cutting decorative shapes from folded paper. The Mola and Kantha quilts are both designs inspired by an ethnic tradition. The Sashiko quilt, in the formal Japanese style, with its precise, geometric patterns is for those who like formal arrangements. There are also two American-style quilts: the block quilt and the traditional nineteenth-century stenciled quilt design. For the more adventurous, the painted and printed quilts provide plenty of freedom to introduce your own designs. Techniques such as felt-making, painting and printing fabric expand the quiltmaker's field, bringing adventure to the design of more individual quilts. Within most sections there is a paragraph suggesting design variations. Each quilt will be individual, so enjoy choosing the quilt that will be just right for you.

HEXAGON QUILT

TO PLAN AND DESIGN YOUR QUILT

Decide on the size of your quilt, the size of the hexagons and a source for the colour of the quilt. Draw a continuous layout of hexagons: They should be the smallest size you can sew together successfully and the layout should extend to fit within the area of the quilt. It could be a quilt 6 x 8 in, made of hexagons with sides measuring ¼ in. This would use 15 x 18 hexagons, with a shaped border made by the natural honeycomb layout of the hexagons or an edge made straight by adding portions of hexagons to fill the spaces. You should use three-sided portions of the hexagons on two opposite sides and two-sided portions of the hexagons on the other two sides. Alternatively, to make the straight edge to the quilt illustrated opposite, the hexagon patchwork is applied to a rectangle of fabric. Make a decision on which edge you prefer, and draw this round the layout of hexagons to complete your quilt plan. The plan is then ready to color, based on your chosen source idea. The colors in the quilt illustrated were inspired by a bed of heather.

MATERIALS NEEDED

small scraps of lawn

cartridge paper

plastic template material – home-made or purchased

sewing thread to tone

interlining (if required)

rectangle of cotton lawn to back the quilt

rectangle of cotton lawn for border

sewing tools

compass

TO MAKE HEXAGON PIECES

To make a hexagon template of the correct size, use a compass to draw a circle with a radius the same length as one of the sides of the required hexagon. With the compass set at the same width, place its point anywhere on the circle and make a mark where the pencil crosses the circumference. Next, move the compass point to this mark and continue in the same way round the circle until six marks have been made. Join the marks with straight lines to form a hexagon. The hexagon may then be traced carefully onto plastic and cut out to make a strong template.

Cut out the required number of hexagons in thick paper – cartridge paper is ideal. Next, cut out hexagons from the lawn in colours matching your design, remembering to add approximately ⅛ in for a seam all round. Pin the paper hexagon in the centre of the fabric shape, with the fabric wrong side up. Turn the extra fabric over the edge of the paper hexagon and tack in place to make a patch as described on page 21.

TO JOIN THE PATCHES AND ADD A BORDER

Join two patches together by placing them face to face and oversewing by hand along one side. Continue to join the patches in this way, folding them occasionally so that they can easily be held during sewing, until the patchwork design is complete. Make quite sure that all fastenings on and off are securely held. The patches may be joined together in rows, or in rosettes as in the quilt illustrated. If a large number of hexagon pieces is used a pin board may be handy (see page 20).

To add a straight border to the hexagon top, place it centrally onto a rectangle of the border fabric, then pin, tack and hem it into place. Cut away the border fabric from behind the hexagons and carefully remove the papers from the hexagons. Press the completed quilt top.

TO MAKE THE QUILT

Make the quilt sandwich as described on page 25, then quilt or knot it as appropriate. I have knotted this quilt with French knots in the centre of the rosettes (see Fig. 5a–c on page 24) because I felt that quilting through all the layers of fabric of the turned sections would be difficult, and that the ends of the traditional quilting knot would look fussy and be a distraction on the quilt surface. The edges can then be sewn together by slip stitching the top to the back, or you can run a quilting stitch right round the edge. If you are making a shaped edge then you will need to turn in the edge of the back carefully to match the shapes of the top, clipping the seam allowance where necessary to keep the shapes clean and sharp. This is quite a difficult job.

VARIATIONS

The different colored hexagons can be arranged in a variety of ways to make many quilt top designs. They could be organized into rosettes, stripes, diagonals or zigzags, a wash of color could be made across the top from dark to light or pale to bright, or the colors could be arranged formally. Fig. 6 will give you some ideas. Any geometric shapes can be assembled in the same way and any ordered combination of the shapes would give a structure to the design.

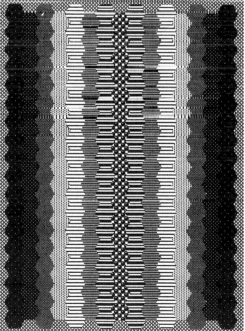

Fig. 6
Hexagon quilt layouts

PAINTED QUILT

TO PLAN AND DESIGN YOUR QUILT

Silk painting is used to decorate the fabric for this quilt, allowing the opportunity to create a unique design. There are many books that give good descriptions on the main characteristics of the technique. The atmospheric qualities of silk painting are very organic and this made me choose the subject of a country landscape for my quilt. The quilt illustrated is 6 x 8 in.

For your plan, draw a rectangle the required size and within it paint a design using watercolor paints. Keep the idea simple but rich in color and with contrasts in tone.

MATERIALS NEEDED

a thin silk (e.g. habutai)

silk paints

water-based gutta

brushes

a small wooden frame

drawing pins with fine points

sewing thread and tools

backing fabric

pencil and ruler

TO PAINT THE QUILT TOP

Before you begin, wash the silk gently. Draw the rectangle of the quilt onto the silk, allowing enough border all round to pin it to the frame. Paint lines of gutta round the shapes of the design. Let these lines dry and then flood the areas between the lines with silk paints. The paints may be diluted with water to make paler colors or intermixed to make a wide range of colors. I do not complete the painting in one go, but fix the colors according to the manufacturer's instructions and then wash the silk and let it dry. I then continue adding gutta lines and silk paints, fixing and washing until I have created the desired design.

TO MAKE THE QUILT

Trim the silk top, leaving enough fabric all round to make the required edge. Make a quilt sandwich and prepare a suitable edge. Finally, quilt the sandwich, perhaps adding more detail to the design. The quilt illustrated is quite delicate because it has no interlining and the silk from the top is taken over onto the back. As a result, it feels more like a bedspread than a quilt.

OTHER TECHNIQUES AND MATERIALS

There are many dyes and pigments on the market today that can be used to color fabric, acrylic paints being just one example. The use of salt with some of the paints will give interesting effects, while any of the traditional resist-dying techniques are very intriguing processes which give amazing results. A list of reference books, which cover some of these exciting methods, is provided on page 110.

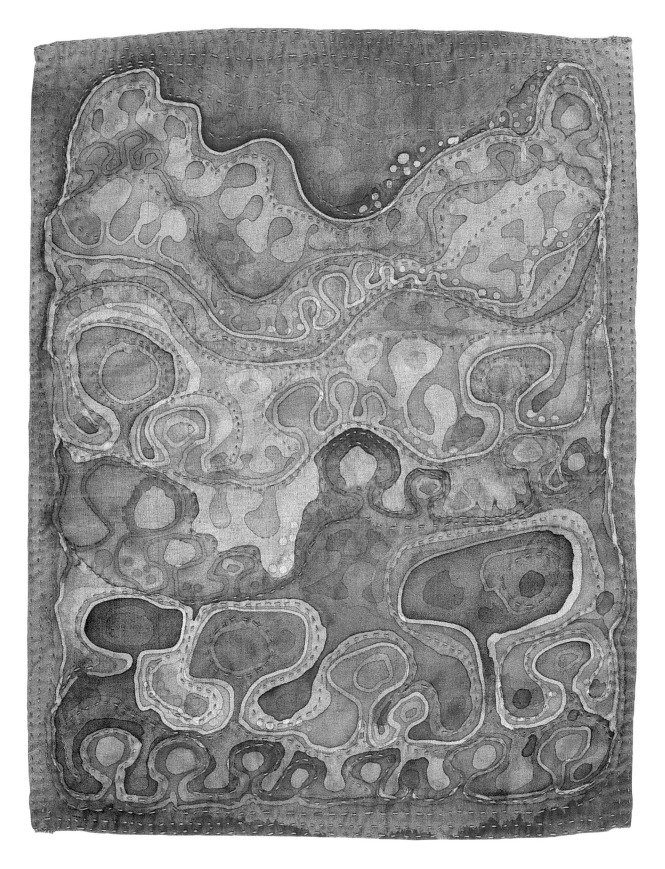

LOG CABIN QUILT

TO PLAN AND DESIGN YOUR QUILT

Decide on the size of your quilt, the size of the log cabin blocks and a color source. The fascinating layout of log cabin quilts is dependent on the use of contrasting colors, such as red and green or on the contrasts of dark and light tones.

First draw a grid of squares, each square the same size as your blocks and the layout extending to the size of the quilt – for example, a 6 x 8 in quilt made of 1 in blocks. Next, draw a square within the center of each grid square ¼ in smaller than the grid square, then a square within this square ¼ in smaller, continuing until you have a ¼ in square in the center. Add lines to connect the squares as shown in Fig. 7 on page 36. This is your quilt plan and is ready to color based on your chosen source idea. The quilt illustrated was inspired by a picture of the squares and angles of a building, blue and brown forming the contrasting sides.

MATERIALS NEEDED

scraps of fine cotton lawn in contrasting
   tones or colours
fine white cotton lawn
sewing thread and tools
pencil and ruler
masking tape
cotton lawn to back the quilt
thin interlining (optional)

TO MAKE A LOG CABIN BLOCK

Use the method of sewing pieces onto a backing fabric (see page 22). Cut a square of white cotton lawn the size of the block plus a ⅛ in seam allowance. Onto this square trace the square of the block directly off your plan, securing your fabric and the plan to a table top with masking tape. Place a scrap of lawn slightly larger than the central square in the center of the white cotton square on its unmarked side. Place a strip of fabric slightly wider than the blocks round the center, face to face with the small square. Using the lines as a guide, use running stitch to sew a straight seam on one side of the square through all three layers of fabric from the marked side. Turn the strip over into place and trim off the excess length. Add strips in this way, on each side of the square, to complete the first round.

Continue in the same direction, adding two more rounds of strips and following the colors in your plan. Use two strips of one color or tone and then two of another to complete each block. Make as many blocks as are needed.

TO JOIN THE BLOCKS

Place two blocks face to face and sew together with a running stitch along the seam line. Open out the seam and press flat. Join other blocks together in the same way to make a row. To complete the quilt, join rows of blocks by placing them face to face and sewing in the same manner.

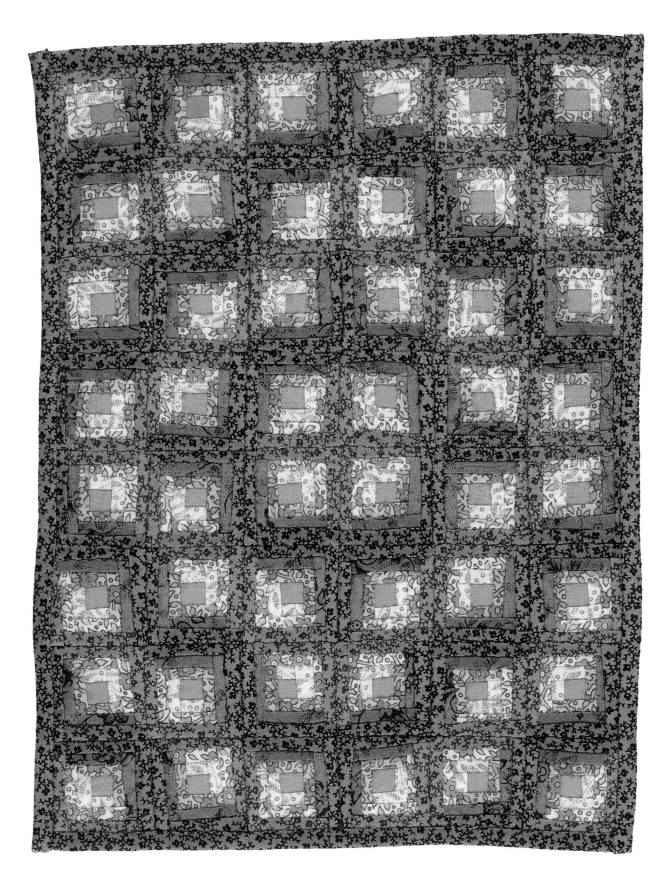

TO MAKE THE QUILT

Cut a piece of cotton lawn the same size as the
quilt top, and the same for an interlining if
required. This technique does not need an
interlining because the patchwork was worked on
cotton lawn, which gives adequate support. Make
the quilt sandwich as described on page 25. Knot or
quilt the sandwich to keep the layers secure and
finish the edge as appropriate (the quilt illustrated
has a straight bound edge).

VARIATIONS

Many variations in the layout of the quilt can be
made by making the required number of blocks and
then moving them around to find the different
layouts possible. See Fig. 8 for more examples.

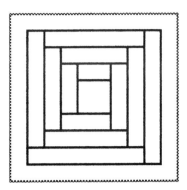

Fig. 7
Log cabin structure

Fig. 8
Variations on the log cabin layout

BLOCK QUILT

TO PLAN AND DESIGN YOUR QUILT

If you choose to make a tree block quilt, decide on the size of your quilt, the size of the tree blocks and a source for the color of the quilt. Inspiration could come from a collection of green- or autumn-colored fabrics or the colors from a photograph taken on holiday. The quilt illustrated was based on winter conifers.

First draw a grid of squares with lattice borders in between each square and round the outside: This could be a quilt 5⅞ x 7¼ in made of 1 in blocks with ⅛ in borders. Draw the trees within the squares; use a triangle that touches three sides of the square and draw two lines from the base of this triangle to the lower edge of the square to represent the trunk. Each tree can be exactly the same or each one different. This is your quilt plan and is ready to color based on your chosen source idea.

MATERIALS NEEDED

fine cotton lawn scraps

print or plain lawn for borders

fine white cotton lawn

sewing thread and tools

pencil

masking tape

TO MAKE TREE BLOCKS

To make the tree blocks, use the method of sewing pieces onto a backing fabric (see page 22). Cut a square of white cotton lawn the size of a tree block with a small seam allowance all round. Mark the tree block on the white square. Place a scrap of lawn representing the trunk of the tree on the unmarked side of the white square and then place a scrap of fabric, representing one of the spaces beside the trunk, face to face with the trunk piece. Using the lines as a guide, sew a seam of running stitches through all three layers of fabric from the marked side. Fasten ends securely. Turn this second scrap over into place and add the third piece – representing the space on the other side of the trunk – in the same way. Then add the main body of the tree and the sky pieces to complete the block. (See Fig. 9 for this and other designs and their order of piecing.) Make as many blocks as are required for the quilt top.

TO JOIN THE BLOCKS INTO THE QUILT TOP

Join the blocks into rows with lattice pieces between them. Cut out short lattice pieces the length of each block plus a seam allowance at either end and the width of two seam allowances plus a seam allowance at each side. For the suggested size this would be 1⅛ x ¾ in. Place a lattice piece face to face with the side edge of a block and sew together along the marked seam. Sew another block to the other side of the lattice piece and then sew the butting blocks together using a ladder stitch. Join all the blocks into rows, then join the rows together in the same way with longer lattice pieces. For the suggested size this would be 5½ x ¾ in. Then add the border all round with two pieces top and bottom, and then two pieces either side, to finish the quilt top. For the suggested size this would be 5½ x ¾ in and 7⅞ x ¾ in.

Make the quilt top into a quilt sandwich with a backing and interlining if required, and finish the edge as appropriate to complete the quilt.

QUILTS FROM OTHER BLOCKS

Many traditional blocks make interesting quilts, but you will have to plan each block carefully so that it can be pieced from the reverse onto a foundation fabric as described. It is also possible to sew the pieces together in the traditional block method. In this case any block may be attempted, although small pieces are more easily handled and managed when you have a foundation fabric.

Illustrated in Fig. 9 are blocks that could make interesting quilts, either spaced with lattice borders or with the blocks butted together as in the log cabin quilt. One block can also be arranged in a variety of ways to make a series of quilts based on one theme – see Fig. 10.

Quilt design for shop using a letter 'A'

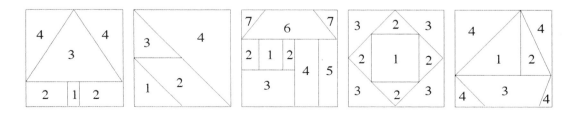

Fig. 9
Block designs in which the piecing order results in interesting quilts

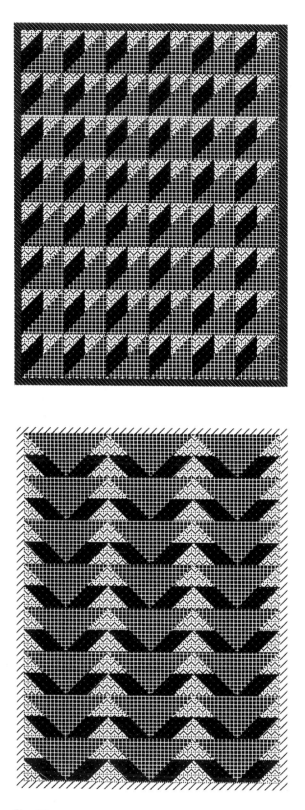

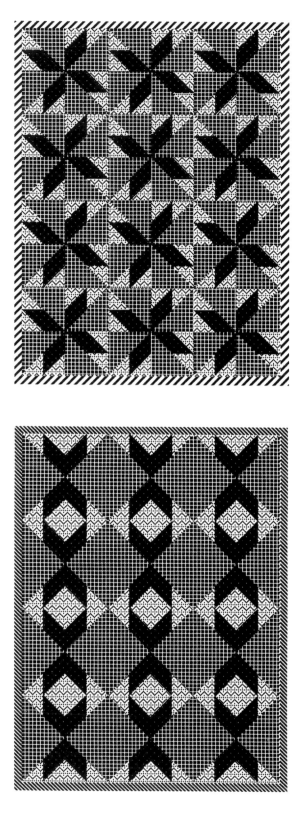

Fig. 10
Layouts showing how one block can be repeated
to make different plans

SUFFOLK PUFF QUILT

TO PLAN AND DESIGN YOUR QUILT

Decide on the size of your quilt, the size of the Suffolk puffs and a source for the color of the quilt. Draw a continuous layout of circles, the circles matching the size of your puffs and the layout extending to the size of the quilt. It could be a quilt 6 x 8 in made of ½ in diameter puffs. This is your quilt plan and is ready to color based on your chosen source idea. The quilt illustrated was based on a picture of ornamental cabbages, the pink bursting out from the center of the greens (see pages 14–15).

MATERIALS NEEDED

   fine cotton lawn
   sewing thread and tools
   circle template

TO MAKE A SUFFOLK PUFF PATCH

Cut out a circle of fine cotton lawn using the circular template. The diameter of the template should be twice that of the finished puff plus two ⅛ in seam allowances of – for example, a template with a diameter of 1¼ in will make a puff with a diameter of ½ in. Turn in the seam allowance round the circle by running a gathering thread through it. Pull up the thread and fasten off securely. Flatten the puff with your fingers to complete it. Make as many puffs as are needed according to your plan.

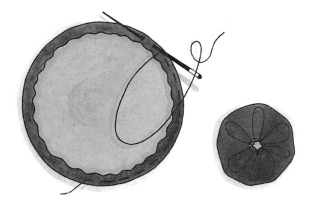

Fig. 11
Making a Suffolk Puff

TO JOIN THE PUFFS

Place two puffs face to face and oversew the edges together for a short distance – this would be approximately ⅛ in for a puff with a ½ in diameter. Open them out flat and join on another puff, continuing in this way to make a row of puffs. Then join the rows together by placing them face to face and oversewing each puff to its neighbour.

TO MAKE THE QUILT

The joined puffs make a very flexible quilt without the need for a backing. However, to give an overall haze of color the quilt may be mounted on cotton lawn by knotting the center of each puff to the backing fabric. The knotting thread can also provide another hint of color.

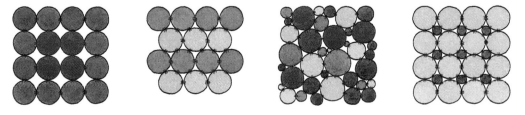

Fig. 12
Four arrangements of Suffolk puffs

ROMAN STRIPES QUILT

TO PLAN AND DESIGN YOUR QUILT

Decide on the size of your quilt, the size of the
Roman stripe blocks and a source for the colour
of the quilt. Draw a grid of squares, each square
the same size as your blocks and the layout
extending to the size of the quilt. It could be a quilt
6 x 8 in, made of 1 in blocks. Draw in the diagonals
of the squares to make two half triangles. In one of
these triangles draw lines parallel with a diagonal
side until the shape is filled. The lines could be
evenly spaced, every ⅛ in. The lines do not need to
go in the same direction from block to block:
Experiment until you find an arrangement that is
pleasing. This is your quilt plan and is ready to
color based on your chosen source idea. Your
colored plan could be cut up into blocks and these
arranged into different patterns – see Fig. 13 for
some ideas.

MATERIALS NEEDED

scraps of fine cotton lawn for the stripes

plain cotton lawn for the triangle

fine white cotton lawn

sewing thread and tools

pencil and ruler

masking tape

cotton lawn to back the quilt

thin interlining (optional)

*Two variations of the Roman stripes
design*

TO MAKE A ROMAN STRIPES BLOCK

To make Roman stripes blocks, use the method of
sewing pieces onto a backing fabric (see page 22).
Cut a square of white cotton lawn to the size of the
block plus a ⅛ in seam allowance. Onto this square
draw the square of the block from your plan. This
can be traced directly off your plan, securing your
fabric and plan to a table top with masking tape.
Place a triangle of plain cotton lawn on half of the
white cotton square on its unmarked side. Place a
strip of fabric face to face with the triangle along
the diagonal of the square, and using the drawn
lines as a guide sew a seam of running stitch
through all three layers of the fabric from the
marked side. Fasten on and off securely. Turn the
strip over into place and trim off the excess length.
Continue to add strips in this way, following the
colors on your plan and filling up the square to
complete the block. (An alternative and easier way
of making a block is with two triangles, one in plain
fabric and the other in striped fabric.) Make as
many blocks as are needed according to your plan.

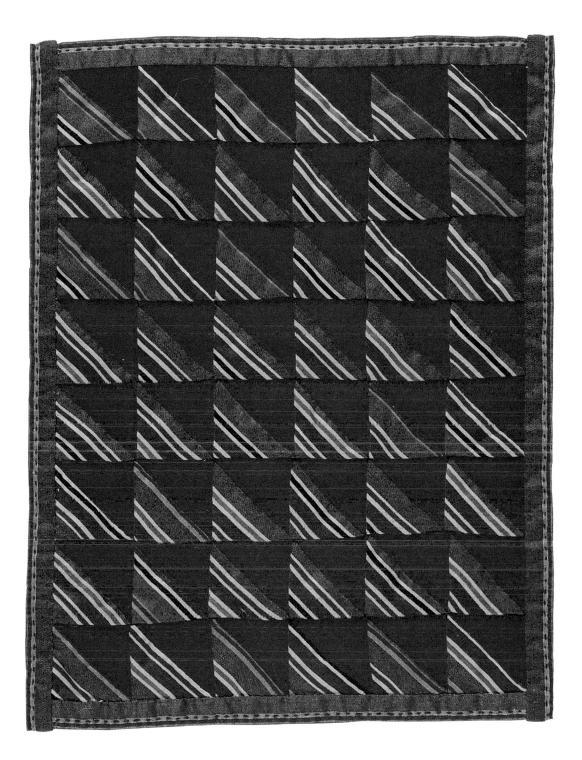

TO JOIN THE BLOCKS

Place two blocks face to face and sew them together with a running stitch along the seam line. Open out the seam and press flat. Join other blocks in the same way to make a row. Join rows of blocks together by placing the rows face to face and sewing in the same manner.

TO MAKE THE QUILT

Construct the quilt with an interlining and a backing fabric if required to make a quilt sandwich as described on page 25. Knot or quilt through the layers to keep them secure and then finish the edge appropriately (the quilt illustrated above has a straight bound edge).

Fig. 13
Variations on the Roman stripe layout

HAWAIIAN QUILT

TO PLAN AND DESIGN YOUR QUILT

Decide on the size of your quilt, the subject and the color. Traditionally, Hawaiian quilts are bright red or green on a white background, but any two contrasting colors will have the same effect and show off the design well. Draw an outline the size of the quilt on white paper and cut out a thin, colored piece of paper to the same size. For a rectangular quilt, fold the colored paper in half and then into quarters. For a square quilt, fold it in half, then into quarters and eighths. Draw a line from one folded edge to the other folded edge. Cut along this line through all layers of the folded paper. Unfold to reveal the design shape (see Fig. 14). Work away at more cut-outs until you are satisfied, then stick it on the white paper to complete the design. The quilts illustrated on page 49 are based on the curving leaves of a hosta plant.

Fig. 14
Making a one-piece cut pattern

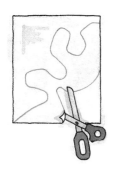
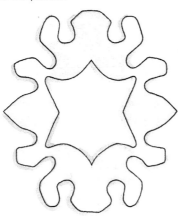

MATERIALS NEEDED

plain cotton lawn for background
cotton lawn for cut-out
tacking thread
sewing thread to tone and tools
interlining
cotton to back the quilt

TO APPLY THE DESIGN

Cut out your fabric design using the same method for working out the design in paper, remembering to add a seam allowance if required. Fold creases into the background fabric in the same way as for the paper cut-out. Unfold the background fabric and place the cut out that is being applied on the background fabric, matching the folds. Then apply the cut-out using any of the basic methods of appliqué (see page 23).

TO MAKE THE QUILT

First iron the quilt top from the back, being careful not to flatten the work too much: the slight raised effect of the piece is attractive. Cut a backing fabric for the quilt and interlining if required. Make the quilt sandwich, then quilt and finish the edge as appropriate to complete the quilt. The quilt illustrated has a turned-in edge. Traditionally, an Hawaiian quilt would have contour quilting lines round the design.

EASY METHODS

The use of fusible webbing makes appliqué more simple and quick, but always remember that it is not strong enough for hard use if used alone – stitching should be added to make it more durable.

Another method to obtain a clean, clear design is to place a sheer fabric such as organdy or organza over the cut design as an additional layer in the quilt sandwich. Keep the design in place by running a quilting stitch round the outline, illustrated above.

Three variations of the Hawaiian quilt design

KANTHA QUILT

TO PLAN AND DESIGN YOUR QUILT

Decide on the size of your quilt – for example, 6 x 8 in. The quilt illustrated is 7½ x 10 in and consists of the borders and triangle shapes found in the Kantha quilts of Bangladesh. First draw an outline of the quilt to size. Within it draw a block of squares with borders between the squares and round the edge. Divide the squares with their diagonals. This is the basic layout for your quilt plan. The feel of the complete quilt may be achieved by drawing dashed lines round the shapes and along the borders: the dashes group together in various ways to form patterns and create a Kantha look.

MATERIALS NEEDED

   soft natural cotton for the top and
      back of the quilt
   colored sewing thread
   pencil
   sewing tools

TO PREPARE AND MAKE THE QUILT SANDWICH

Draw the basic quilt layout onto the top fabric with a pencil. Cut out a backing fabric and make the quilt sandwich as described on page 25.

Traditionally full-size Kantha quilts are made from many layers of old sari fabric. Although two layers are enough for a miniature quilt you may add more to make a firmer quilt if this is appropriate.

TO MAKE THE QUILT

Following the pencil markings on the quilt top, quilt round the edge of the triangles and the borders. Starting at the outside of each shape, work continuous rows of quilting round and round in colored thread until the shape is filled. Quilt along the borders, staggering the stitches to make different patterns. The color can be changed as often as you like to suit your design. Finish with rows of quilting round the edge and remove the tacking.

VARIATIONS

Instead of using triangles, the quilt can be covered with different shapes that are arranged freely and surrounded by a final border. Colored elephants, fish and everyday objects are often seen on the traditional quilts, together with the border patterns and free contour lines of quilting in neutral colors to fill the background.

Although there is no easy way to imitate the charming quality of traditional Kantha work, this simple technique gives a feel for the style.

WHOLECLOTH QUILT

TO PLAN AND DESIGN YOUR QUILT

Decide on the size of your quilt. It could be
6 x 8 in and made of white or plain colors with a
small-print fabric backing in the style of a
traditional British quilt. Fig. 15 illustrates some of
the traditional quilted patterns used in Welsh and
North Country quilts. Next, decide on the layout.
The quilt illustrated is in the style of a Welsh quilt,
with a central medallion, a border round the edge
and an infilling pattern between. Draw an outline
of the quilt to size and within it draw the lines of
the layout. You can then add the individual patterns
to complete your plan. This is then ready to be
transferred to the quilt top (see photograph on page
22).

MATERIALS NEEDED

fine pale plain cotton lawn for the
    top of the quilt
interlining
fine cotton lawn to back the quilt
sewing thread to match
sewing tools
pencil
masking tape

TO PREPARE AND MAKE THE QUILT SANDWICH

Secure the plan to a table and place the quilt top
fabric over it. Trace the plan on to the fabric with a
pencil. Cut a backing fabric and interlining, then
make the quilt sandwich (see page 25) and prepare
the edge as appropriate (this would traditionally be
a butted edge).

TO MAKE THE QUILT

Following the pencil pattern marks, quilt your
design. Start from the center and finish with a
double row of quilting round the edge. Remove the
tacking to complete the quilt.

VARIATIONS

Another traditional style is the 'strippy' quilt. Use
plain-colored strips pieced together and quilt with
traditional patterns that repeat down the quilt from
top to bottom along the strips.

Fig. 15
Traditional wholecloth patterns

EASY METHOD

There is not an easy way to imitate the wholecloth quilt, but it is possible to machine the quilt lines using a fine or invisible thread on the top that hides the hard line of the machine stitch. The machine stitch will make the quilt stiff and the ends of threads will need to be sewn back into the sandwich (a time-consuming process which makes hand-stitching seem easy).

SOMERSET STAR QUILT

TO PLAN AND DESIGN YOUR QUILT

Decide on the size of your quilt, the size of the
Somerset Star Blocks and a source for the color of the
quilt. Draw a layout of squares with a border
between the squares. Twelve 1 in blocks with ½ in
borders would make a 5 x 6½ in quilt. Draw the
diagonals and the quarter lines into each square. This
is your quilt plan and is ready to color. Do this by
sticking colored paper triangles onto the plan. Four
of these can be cut from 1 in squares of colored
papers according to your chosen source idea. Design
your colored stars by sticking the triangles onto the
squares of the quilt plan, lining them up with the
quarter and diagonal lines and then overlapping
them. Starting at the center, arrange them round the
square until it is covered. The blocks can all be the
same or can be varied; the quilt illustrated was based
on the color of a favorite fabric print.

MATERIALS NEEDED

    fine cotton lawn squares
    printed or plain cotton lawn for the
        lattice and borders
    fine white cotton lawn for the
        foundation squares
    cotton lawn to back the quilt
    thin interlining (optional)
    masking tape
    sewing thread and tools
    pencil and ruler

Fig. 16a–d
Making a Somerset patch

Fig. 16a

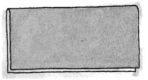

Fig. 16b

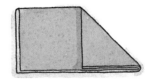

Fig. 16c

Fig. 16d

TO MAKE A SOMERSET PATCH

Fold the small squares of colored cotton in half horizontally, then fold the creased corners down to meet each other. This makes a right-angled triangular patch with all the raw edges at the base (see Fig. 16a–d). It is important that the folds are sharp and accurate. Press them using a damp cloth. For the suggested size I used 1 in squares.

TO APPLY THE PATCHES

Mark with a pencil and ruler or iron the quarter and diagonal lines on the foundation fabric squares (Fig. 17a). For the suggested size, these are 1½ in square with a ¼ in seam allowance. Place a folded patch with its point in the center of this square, using the lines as a guide. Anchor the point down with a single stitch at its center. Sew down the raw edge of the patch using a running or a hem stitch (see Fig. 17b).

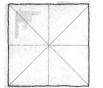

Fig. 17a
Guide lines marked on the foundation square

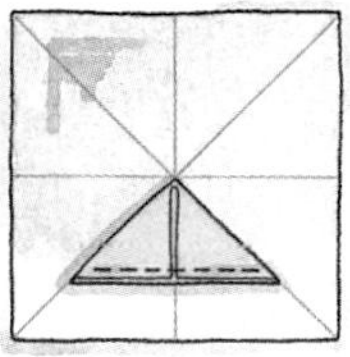

Fig. 17b
First patch sewn in place

Sew three more patches into the center to complete a square (see Fig. 17c). Take eight patches and pin them around the first four, four centered on the quarter lines and four on the diagonals, to complete the round (see Fig. 17d).

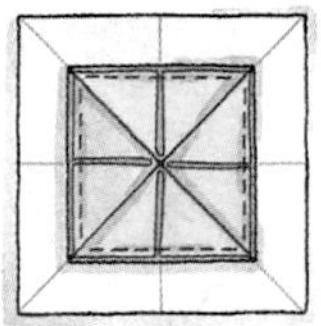

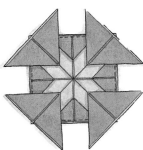

Fig. 17c
First round of patches sewn in place

Fig. 17d
Final patches in place

Each patch is placed using the guide lines and pulled away from the center. To ensure even overlapping, the patches need to be worked in opposite pairs. Carefully sew the points into place

first followed by the raw edges, hiding the raw edges of the first four patches. Trim the final patches to the edge of the foundation square. This completes the block (see Fig. 17e). Make as many blocks as necessary.

Fig. 17e
Final patches trimmed to complete the block

TO JOIN THE BLOCKS

Join the blocks into rows with lattice pieces between them. Cut out lattice pieces the length of the blocks plus a seam allowance on either end, and the width of two seam allowances plus a seam allowance on each side. For the suggested size this would be 1 x 1½ in. Place a lattice piece face to face with the side edge of a block and sew them together along the seam line. Sew another block to the other side of the lattice piece and then sew the butting blocks together using a ladder stitch. Join the rows in the same way with longer lattice pieces; for the suggested size this would be 1 x 6 in. Complete the top of the quilt by adding border pieces either side and then top and bottom – for the suggested size this would be 1 x 6 in and 1 x 5½ in. In the quilt illustrated I added an extra border to bring the quilt up in size.

TO MAKE THE QUILT

Construct the quilt with a backing and interlining (if needed). Knot or quilt to keep the layers secure. Finish the edge appropriately. The quilt illustrated has a butted edge, is knotted with toning beads and is quilted round the border and edge.

CRAZY QUILT

TO PLAN AND DESIGN YOUR QUILT

Decide on the dimensions of your quilt and divide it up into shapes; these do not need to be square but it would make the construction of the quilt easier if they can be sewn together without having to sew round corners. The quilt could measure 6 x 8 in and be made up in any number of layouts, such as one of those illustrated in Fig. 18 overleaf. Draw the shape of the quilt and the divisions to make your basic plan, which is then ready to colour with crazy shapes based on your chosen source idea. The quilt illustrated was based on the layout of a traditional strippy quilt and the colours of a traditional Victorian crazy cover, in which odd scraps of fabric left over from other projects were assembled and then embellished with beads, sequins, motifs and embroidery.

MATERIALS NEEDED

scraps of fine fabric

plain cotton lawn for patchwork foundation

sewing thread and tools

fabric to back the quilt

thin interlining (optional)

braid or ribbon

sequins and beads

fusible webbing

TO MAKE A CRAZY PATCHWORK

Draw the chosen layout of the quilt onto plain cotton and apply a fusible webbing, following the manufacturer's instructions. Cut out the shapes of the basic layout and use these as the foundation for the patchwork. Remove the paper backing from the webbing. Completely cover the layout shapes with small, random shapes of colored fabric, pressing down onto the webbing with your hand as you work. The warmth of your hand will hold the pieces in place until the shape is completely covered. Press with a warm iron and damp cloth. Add any embroidery at this stage. It is advisable to embroider round each piece to keep it secure. This can be done with colored sewing thread; yellow was a favorite with the Victorians for this purpose. A variety of stitches were commonly used, such as the herringbone stitch I used here, or buttonhole, blanket, feather or any other decorative stitch.

An alternative method of making the crazy patchwork is to work in the method described on page 22 for sewing pieces onto a backing fabric. The small pieces in this method would have their edges turned under, and so the embroidery round each piece would not be necessary and a plainer quilt would result.

TO JOIN THE SHAPES

Join together the shapes now covered with crazy pieces with a ladder stitch, making a neat, flat seam. Join on other shapes in the same way, keeping the work flat by avoiding sewing round corners if possible.

TO FINISH THE QUILT TOP

Cover the ladder stitching along the seams by applying a braid or ribbon. Apply more round the edge, enhancing the effect with lace if desired.

TO MAKE THE QUILT

Construct the quilt as described on page 25, knotting or quilting to keep the layers secure. Add embellishments in the form of more embroidery, sequins, beads and bows, to evoke the highly fancy and sometimes sparkly feel of the Victorian era. The sequins and beads can also be used practically to knot the layers together.

Fig. 18
Layout plans for crazy quilts

PRINTED QUILT

TO PLAN AND DESIGN YOUR QUILT

Basic potato prints can be used to make attractive cloths for quilts. Decide on a simple motif for a design and also its size. The quilt illustrated here is 6 x 8 in, while the motifs have been printed on it within the squares of a 1 in grid. Draw a rectangle to the required size of your quilt with an appropriate measured grid to act as guide lines.

Next make an experimental cut from a potato and try out your print (the motif on the example was based on the spiral quilting patterns found on Welsh quilts). Slice a potato in half and cut into the flat surface to form the chosen motif. The raised parts that remain form the printing surface. To make a colored design, paint the printing surface and press it down onto the paper within the rectangle, following the grid as a guide. Continue in this way until the design is worked out. A number of different patterns can be made from just one simple motif.

MATERIALS NEEDED

    plain cotton
    fabric paints and fabric pens (optional)
    brushes
    a sharp knife
    a potato
    masking tape
    sewing thread and tools
    batting (optional)
    backing fabric

TO PRINT THE QUILT TOP

Wash the fabric before printing, then fix it on your work surface with masking tape. Draw the rectangle and the grid lightly on the fabric. Using the original potato motif or making a new, similar one, print the fabric using fabric paints according to your design. Let the print dry and then fix the paint according to the manufacturer's instructions. I added lines with a fabric pen on the illustrated quilt at this stage.

TO MAKE THE QUILT

Trim the top, leaving enough fabric to allow for the required edge. Make a quilt sandwich and prepare a suitable edge. Quilt the sandwich, enhancing the design with your stitching. The quilt illustrated has a thin interlining which is usually used for garments that need firmness but little bulk. Finish the edge to complete the quilt.

OTHER TECHNIQUES AND MATERIALS

Experiment by printing with other vegetables and with a variety of objects. A print tool can be made from anything which can form a raised surface: leaves from the garden and old cotton reels are both suitable printing vehicles. There are also many dyes and pigments on the market that can be used to color fabric. The Further Reading section on page 110 lists books that give more information on other printing techniques and materials.

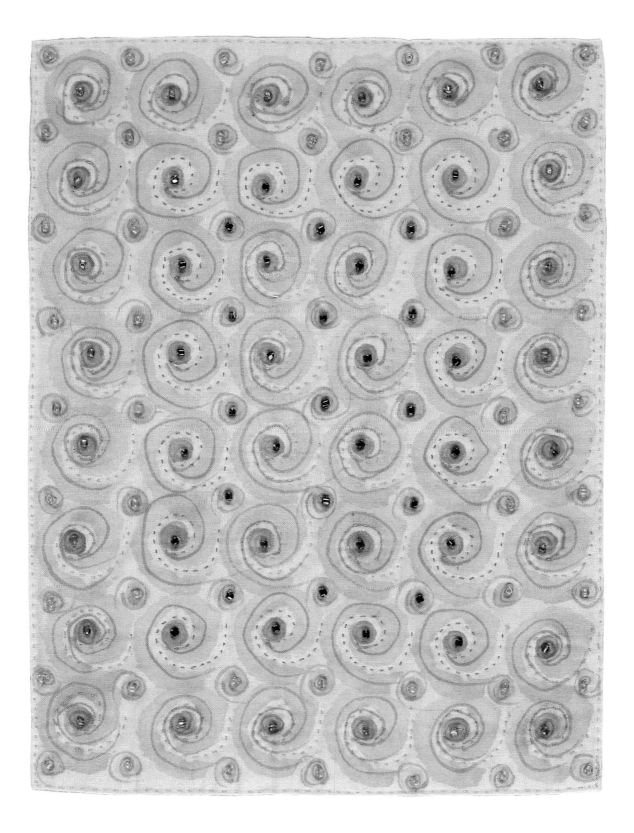

APPLIQUÉ QUILT

TO PLAN AND DESIGN YOUR QUILT

Decide on the size of your quilt, the subject and the overall color. Draw an outline the size of the quilt and roughly draw your ideas within this shape. This can be done by cutting out or tearing shapes from an old magazine to make a collage and then penning fine lines on top. Remember to ensure the shapes you use are in a scale that suits the miniature. The design could be based on traditional ideas, such as a basket of flowers, a cornucopia of fruit or a wreath of seasonal foliage. Fill your space well and make sure that you plan the spaces around the design as well as the subject itself. The quilt illustrated is 6 x 8 in with a ¼ in border and is based on a traditional design of a bowl of flowers.

MATERIALS NEEDED

background fabric

small scraps of lawn with interesting
    printed motif details

tacking thread

sewing thread to tone

sewing tools

interlining

cotton lawn to back the quilt and for border

TO APPLY THE DESIGN

Cut out motifs and compile your design as in the broderie perse style, in which shapes are cut from printed fabric and then reassembled and applied onto another fabric. Apply the pieces as described on page 23.

TO MAKE THE QUILT

First iron the quilt top from the back, being careful not to flatten the work too much. Cut out a backing fabric and interlining, then make the quilt sandwich. Finish the edge as appropriate (the quilt illustrated has a straight bound edge).

VARIATIONS

The number of variations for appliqué quilts is endless as any subject can be illustrated by the technique. Plain and printed fabrics can be shaped, or the background fabric can be pieced from regular shapes and then others applied.

EASY METHODS

The use of fusible webbing makes the method of applying minute pieces more simple and quick. But always remember that the use of webbing alone is not strong enough for hard wear such as a child might give to a doll's quilt; stitching should be added to make it more serviceable. Another method to obtain a clean, clear design is to use a sheer fabric such as organdy or organza as an additional layer over the top of a cut-out design. These pieces are then kept in place by running a quilting stitch round each outline.

FELT QUILT

TO PLAN AND DESIGN YOUR QUILT

This quilt is based on the idea of making felt from carded colored wool 'tops' and mohair yarns. Felt is simple to make using any number of different colors. First make a colored plan the size of the finished quilt, based on an idea which gives you both color and linear structure. An ideal subject for inspiration is rock strata. The quilt illustrated is 6 x 8 in, and was based on a view of a cliff. You could use watercolor paint to represent the overall color of your design and colored pencils to draw in the linear aspects.

MATERIALS NEEDED

    dyed, carded and combed wool

    small lengths of mohair yarn

    plain curtain netting

    warm soap suds

    rush mat

    rolling pin

    coloured sewing thread and sewing tools

    iron

TO MAKE THE QUILT

Work on a plastic top. Lay out the curtain netting and on this make a fine layer of the carded wool, with all the fibers lying in one direction and covering an area a fraction bigger all round than the expected size of the quilt. Place a second layer of wool on top of the first running in the opposite direction, and then a third in the first direction. The colors of the wool can vary throughout the quilt, or each layer can be different, according to your design. Lay threads of the mohair yarn over the top layer. Fold the netting over the pile of wool and wet all the way through with warm soap suds. Compress the pile with your fingers and then create a felt by moving your fingertips in a circular motion. As soon as bobbles of wool come through the netting, pull the netting off and turn the felt over, making sure the edges are not too straggly by pushing them into a neat shape. Continue to create a felt as before. Shrink the felt by rolling it up over a rolling pin, first in one direction and then in the opposite. To complete the felting, give it a good hot iron and leave to dry. To complete the quilt, add quilting lines for detail and strength.

This is a useful method for making miniature rugs and blankets. There are also many different ways of adding detail to the felt. Commercially produced felt can be cut into regular shapes and added to the layers of wool or applied to a base piece of felt. Experiment with various materials to see what can be incorporated into a piece of felt.

MOLA QUILT

TO PLAN AND DESIGN YOUR QUILT

Decide on the size of your quilt, the subject and a choice of bright colors. Draw an outline the size of the quilt and roughly draw your animal or animals within this shape. Try to draw your motif with a single, continuous line and include all features. This will give you a simple, child-like drawing which is appropriate for this style of appliqué. Fill your spaces with extra lines and shapes, and add details such as the eyes. The quilt illustrated is 6 x 8 in and incorporates a fish motif.

MATERIALS NEEDED

> background fabric
> small scraps of brightly coloured cotton lawn
> tacking thread
> sewing thread to tone
> sewing tools

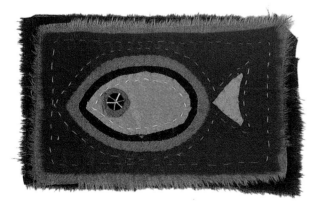

TO WORK REVERSE APPLIQUÉ

Assemble three or more layers of different colored, plain, lightweight cotton lawns. Cut away the basic shape or shapes from the design and use these as templates to mark the top layer. Tack all layers together approximately ¼ in round the outside of each shape. Cut away the shapes through the first layer only and remove. Apply the cut edge by hemming with a matching thread, turning under as you proceed. Cut away the next layer and apply. Continue in this way through the layers, revealing more colors but leaving the back layer uncut. The shapes that have been removed can be cut into, and replaced within, the shape. Alternatively, slits can be made in another part of the top layer and small pieces of coloured lawn placed underneath. These are then hemmed down. Continue decorating the top in this way, removing shapes and replacing the cut shapes or introducing new colors until the design is complete. In the quilt illustrated I used three layers, cutting away two in the basic shape of the fish to reveal the black of the backing fabric. I then added extra colors within the body shapes and a tail shape outside the basic shapes, so that each fish was different.

TO MAKE THE QUILT

The layers can be quilted together with different colored sewing threads to enhance the animals. I have added sequins for the eyes of the fish. Iron the quilt top from the back, being careful not to

flatten the work too much. There is no need to add
any more layers to the quilt as it already consists of
a sandwich. Finally, finish the edge as appropriate
to complete the quilt. The edges of the fish quilt
have been cut to reveal all the colored layers and
then left free to fray.

VARIATIONS

You could design a quilt with bold, geometric lines,
imitating a style of design used by the Cuna Indians
of the San Blas Islands off the coast of Panama. Or

what about the scroll shapes characteristic of the
Pa nDau work of north Vietnamese people, when a
simple line is cut in the top layer and the fabric on
either side is then turned under to reveal the colour
of the base fabric?

EASY METHODS

It is possible to cut away the fabric layers without
allowing for turnings, and to then apply the edges
with a herringbone or any other decorative
covering stitch.

QUILT OF SQUARES

TO PLAN AND DESIGN YOUR QUILT

Decide on the size of your quilt, the size of the squares and a source for the color of the quilt. Draw a continuous layout of squares: they should be the smallest size that you can handle successfully when sewing. A quilt measuring 6 x 8 in, made of ½ in squares, will consist of 192 squares. Color your quilt plan based on your chosen source idea. The quilt illustrated was based on a check of light and dark squares and was made from samples of printed cotton fabric that I have accumulated over the years. Other possible layout arrangements are suggested in the computer drawings in Fig. 19 overleaf.

MATERIALS NEEDED

small pieces of fabric
sewing thread to tone
sewing tools
interlining (optional)
cotton lawn to back the quilt
fabric to bind the quilt
pins and pin board
square template
pencil and ruler

TO PIECE THE SQUARES

Make a strong template the size of one square on your plan, with a ⅛ in seam allowance all round and a second template the actual size of the required patch. Cut out the required number of fabric squares using the template that includes the seam allowance. Using the other template, mark with a pencil the seam allowance on the back of the fabric squares. Arrange the squares to your liking. To make it easier to handle the small pieces and so as not to get their positions muddled, I pin the patches onto a small board in the arrangement of the quilt. To join the squares, place two face to face and sew the patches together along one side on the marked seam line. Sew them into rows and then sew the rows together to complete the quilt top.

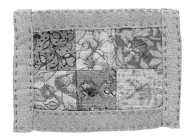

Two variations of the quilt of squares design

TO MAKE THE QUILT

Make the quilt sandwich by first laying the back of the quilt face down, laying the interlining (if required) over this, and then placing the quilt top centrally face up. Pin and tack these together through all layers. Prepare and tack the edge, trimming all layers to match and leaving a seam allowance all round. Prepare the edge as appropriate; this could be a butted edge or a bound edge as in the quilt illustrated. Quilt or knot as appropriate, then finish the edge by hemming or quilting.

Fig. 19a
Variations in the design of a quilt of squares

TUCKED QUILT

TO PLAN AND DESIGN YOUR QUILT

The technique used to make this quilt is to sew with a double needle on a sewing machine, thereby creating raised lines on the surface of the fabric. As the technique is complicated you will need to practise, following the instructions of the machine's manufacturer, before you start to plan the quilt. The quilts illustrated are 6 x 8 in. Draw a rectangle the required size and across it draw a series of lines based on a source idea such as a fence, a brick wall or a landscape of rolling hills. Double all the lines to obtain an idea of how your design will appear. Extra lines, in the form of contour lines round any shapes made by crossing double needle lines, will add interest to the basic design. Keep the idea simple (see Fig. 19b for some ideas). It's best to work on a pale background, using colored threads for the raised lines.

MATERIALS NEEDED

> sewing machine
> pale cotton fabric
> sewing thread
> backing fabric
> pencil

TO MAKE THE QUILT

Cut out the quilt top a fraction larger all round than the required size to allow for the fact that it will shrink slightly after stitching. Draw the basic lines of the design onto the top fabric with a pencil. Stitch along these lines using the double needle. Next, make the quilt sandwich as described on page 25 – I used a lightweight silk for the back of my quilt and no interlining. Prepare the edge as appropriate. The double lines of stitching are bulky, making it difficult to turn the edge under, so I chose to leave the edges free all round the quilt. I then frayed away a few rows of thread from the top and the back fabrics to give a soft appearance. The contour lines can now be quilted by hand, using coloured threads according to the design. The soft quality of the hand-quilting complements the hard machine lines to complete the quilt.

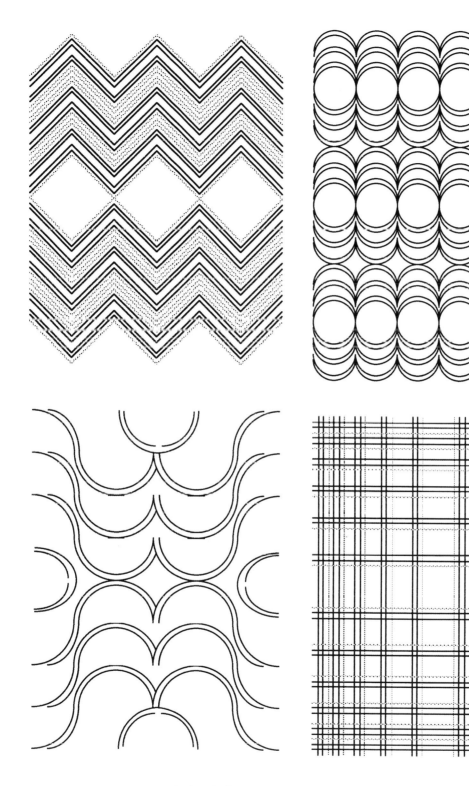

Fig. 19b Variations in a tucked quilt design

CATHEDRAL WINDOW QUILT

TO PLAN AND DESIGN YOUR QUILT

Decide on the size of your quilt, the size of the folded patches and a source for the color of the quilt. Draw a grid of squares, each square the same size as the folded patches and the layout extending to the dimensions of the quilt. Your quilt may measure 6 x 8 in, with 1 in folded patches. Draw in the diagonals of the squares, then place the point of the compass on the center of each side of every square and draw a circle with a radius half the length of the side of a square. Your plan is now ready to color (the quilt illustrated was based on a picture of cosmetic powders).

MATERIALS NEEDED

fine cotton lawn
small scraps of lawn
sewing thread and tools
seed beads (optional)
pencil and ruler

TO MAKE A CATHEDRAL WINDOW PATCH

First cut out a square of plain lawn. This needs to be four times as large as the final patch, plus a seam allowance of ⅛ in. For example, a template of 2¼ in square will make a finished folded patch of 1 in square. Fold in the seam allowance accurately all round (Fig. 20a). This fold may be ironed but do not iron the rest of the folds. Fold the corners into the

middle and secure each with a stitch (Fig. 20b). Fold the new corners to the middle and secure neatly to complete the patch (Fig. 20c). Make as many folded patches as are needed according to your plan.

Fig. 20a

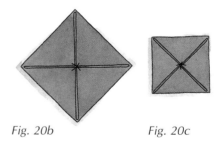

Fig. 20b   *Fig. 20c*

TO JOIN THE PATCHES

Place two patches face to face and oversew together along one side (Fig. 20d). Open them out flat and join more patches to these in the same way, thereby making a row (Fig. 20e). Join the rows together in the same way, making sure that you keep the folded corners neat.

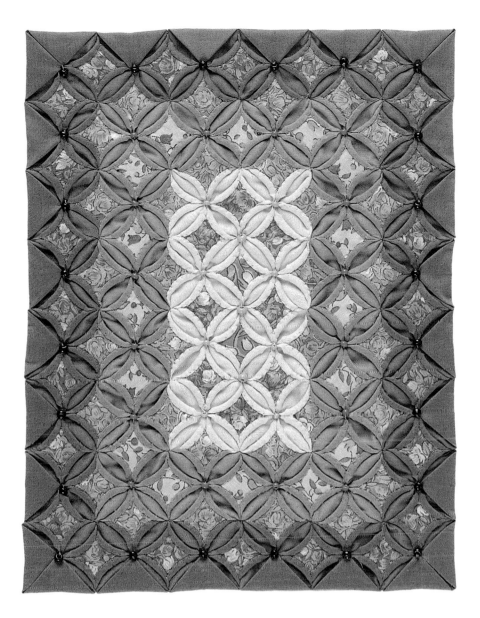

Fig. 20d *Fig. 20e*

Fig. 20f

TO INSERT THE TOP PATCHES

Cut a square of cotton that is slightly smaller than the square formed by the diagonal folds of the joined patches. Pin the square patch into place inside the folded bias edges. Roll the folded bias edges over the square patch and hem down (Fig. 20f).

TO MAKE THE QUILT

This quilt does not need any additional backing but extra embellishments may be added. In the example, seed beads were sewn in at the patch junctions.

KNOTTED QUILT

TO PLAN AND DESIGN YOUR QUILT

The technique of knotting can be combined with the unfraying quality of leather, felt or plastic to make a rich textural surface to a quilt. Knots can be made in a variety of ways: thin or thick strips can be knotted into the surface or extra pieces of material can be held in the knot. Practice drawing knots with different characteristics, scribbling with colored pencils or blobbing with paint. Next, decide on the size of your quilt. The quilt illustrated is 6 x 8 in, with knots arranged in formal lines. Draw a rectangle the required size and into it draw a series of lines. To complete your plan, arrange the knots along these lines.

MATERIALS NEEDED

leather

plastic

felt

coloured thread

hole punch

scissors or knife

pencil and ruler

TO MAKE THE QUILT

For the quilt, base cut out a piece of leather, felt or plastic the actual size of the required quilt. Mark lines on this according to your design and then mark the position of the knots along these lines. Punch two holes in the quilt base at each position of a knot. Cut strips of leather, felt and plastic in the appropriate colours for your design. Thread the strips through the holes and tie reef knots on the surface of the quilt base (see Fig. 4 on page 24). Continue threading and knotting until the surface is covered and the quilt completed according to your design. This makes a very flexible quilt.

VARIATIONS

The simple knots can be arranged in a multitude of layouts. You could use lines crisscrossing the quilt in various grids or groupings of knots in contrasting colors or tones. Knots can be made in a variety of different materials, such as colored embroidery threads, singly or in groups, strips of fabric or any material that is flexible enough to tie a knot in. Another idea is to tie in a bead or sequin with the thread. Combinations of these ideas would make an interesting surface for a quilt.

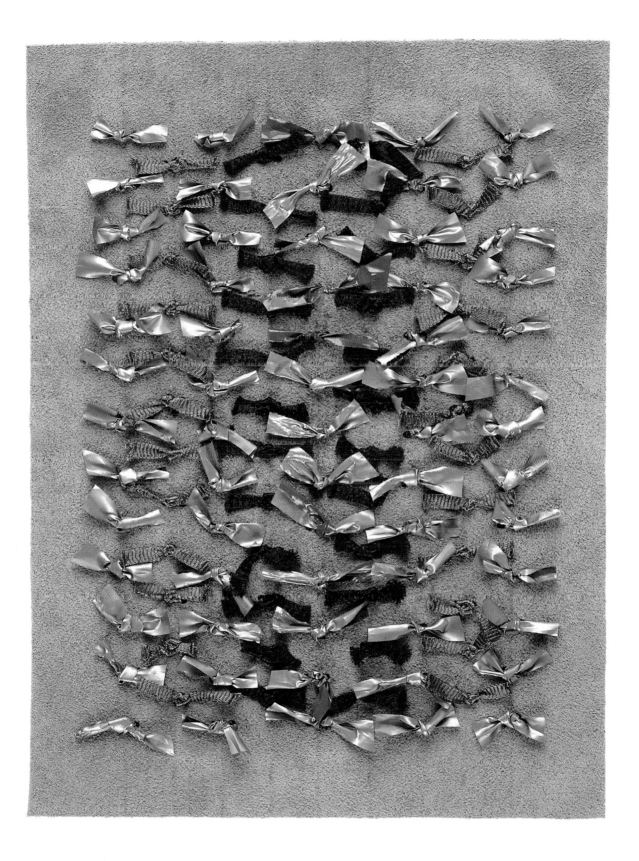

PAPER QUILT

TO PLAN AND DESIGN YOUR QUILT

This quilt is based on the easily available commodity of paper in the form of newsprint, computer paper and old envelopes. Paper that is pulped down and used like modeling clay is called papier mâché. It is made by tearing paper up into small pieces, washing it in boiling water and washing-up liquid to remove any print and then liquidizing and coloring the results. The resulting pulp can be rolled out into a flat sheet when wet and then left to dry. The illustrated quilt measures 6 x 8 in and is based on a grid of squares. Plan the area of your quilt in a tessellation of interlocking shapes with a color scheme in mind. For inspiration look to such things as brickwork and tile shapes. Draw a basic plan and colour according your chosen source idea.

MATERIALS NEEDED

    papier mâché
    dyes or water-based paint
    PVA glue
    rolling pin or press
    beads, sequins, etc., to decorate
    colored threads (optional)

TO MAKE THE QUILT

Squeeze as much water out of the pulp as possible. Divide the pulp into batches and color these with dyes or water-based paints. The batches can then be intermixed to make more colors. Working on a plastic surface, arrange the pulp in the shapes of the design, making sure there are no gaps. Press down with your fingers and then press flat with the rolling pin or a press if available. The end result may be made stronger by adding PVA glue to the pulp or by painting the dried quilt with a dilute solution of PVA glue. Small holes can easily be made in the dried pulp with a needle and then beads, sequins and stitching can all be added to create an interesting surface. The finished quilt will be stiff and will therefore be more suited for use as a wall hanging or floor covering.

VARIATIONS

There are numerous techniques involving paper that could be used in the making of an imaginative quilt. Paper can be torn up and pasted with a dilute PVA glue onto a thinner base paper to produce a fabric-like quality. The resulting materials can then be stitched and treated in the same way as fabric. Any attractive papers, such as sweet wrapping papers, can be applied to a base, and fabric and paper can be used together with sewing, with PVA glue or with both. Experiment with new ideas.

FRAYED QUILT

TO PLAN AND DESIGN YOUR QUILT

This quilt makes use of the effect produced by frayed bias edges. An easy way to show this off is to design a quilt based on squares. The quilt illustrated is a 6 x 8 in rectangle, with the square patches set on their points and a square grid running through the patches from point to point. The colors are arranged round the central line, producing the effect of an oriental rug. Draw a rectangle to the required size and mark on it a square grid. Draw in the diagonal lines of the grid and color this plan, remembering that the quilt will be made from basic squares.

MATERIALS NEEDED

    small pieces of natural-fibre fabric
    backing fabric
    sewing machine
    water-soluble glue
    coloured sewing thread
    interlining (optional)

TO MAKE THE QUILT

The squares are stuck down according to the design with a glue that will wash out. Smaller squares are stuck on top of larger ones to obtain a better blend of color. Run a machine stitch in the form of a grid that passes through all the corners of the small squares, varying the color to co-ordinate with your design. The machine stitch should be as small as the fabric will accommodate. The quilt will look very flat at this stage. Wash the quilt to remove the glue and to loosen the edges so that they will fray. The quilt is now complete, and makes a lightweight covering depending on how many layers of squares have been applied. The quilt may be sandwiched with a backing and an interlining to make it more substantial if required.

VARIATIONS

There are many ways of using the bias edge to allow the threads to fray. Strips cut on the bias can be interwoven to make a fabric like a plaid. They can then be applied to a backing fabric with a line of matching stitching running through the center of each strip. Alternatively, a pile of fabrics can be stitched together with a square grid and a bias cut made across the diagonals of the squares of the grid. Any of these ideas can be combined to present an interesting play of color or a textured surface on a quilt. The work will need to be washed and dried in order to soften the edges.

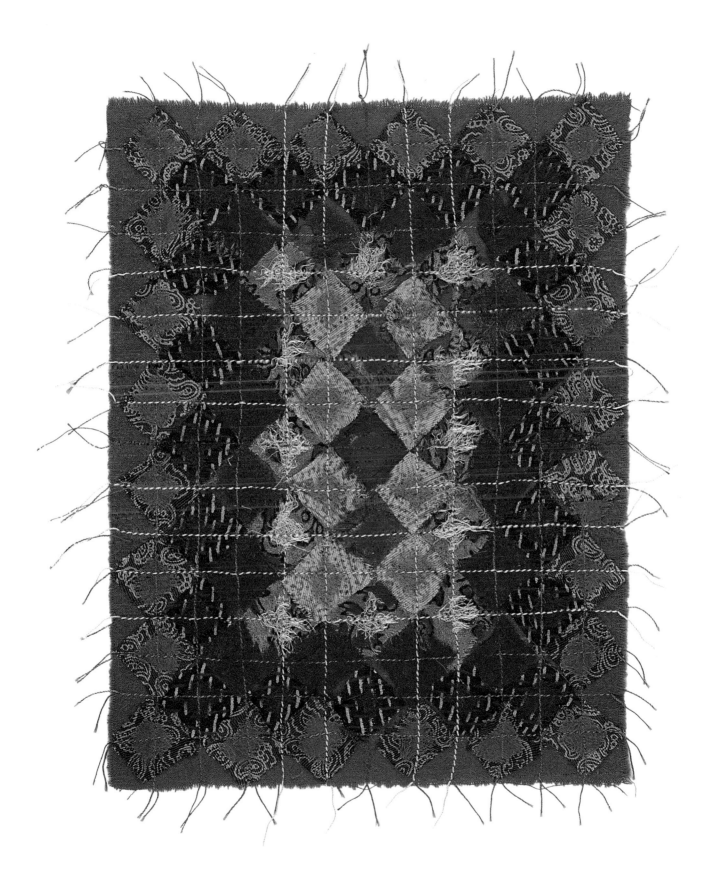

EMBELLISHED QUILT

TO PLAN AND DESIGN YOUR QUILT

An embellished quilt is based on the idea that anything can be applied to a base fabric. This type of quilt will almost design itself when you have assembled a selection of items to apply. These could be things that evoke a memory, a collection of favourite items or items made specially for an individual quilt. Be careful to keep all the items to a suitably small scale. The quilt illustrated is 6 x 8 in, its form based on a section of a woven check from a Madras cotton. The fabric leaves have been decorated with three-dimensional fabric paint, sequins and beads. First draw a rectangle to the required size with a grid to represent your check. Plan the quilt by making various arrangements of your selected items within the grid, changing the arrangement until you are satisfied. Record the placements.

MATERIALS NEEDED

    base fabric of check or plaid
    three-dimensional fabric paint
    beads, sequins, etc.
    backing fabric
    interlining (optional)
    colored sewing threads
    sewing tools

TO MAKE THE QUILT

Apply the items to the base fabric according to your plan, using any of the methods described earlier in the book in the section on appliqué (see page 23). The stitching used can either be serviceable or decorative. Three-dimensional paint can be added at any stage of the work, but remember that the paint cannot be ironed (the three-dimensional paint in the illustrated quilt was applied at the last stage). Beads and sequins can be added after the quilt sandwich has been assembled and used to help hold the sandwich together. The quilt may be sandwiched with a backing and an optional interlining and the edge should be prepared as appropriate – the quilt illustrated has a frayed edge. Quilt and knot the sandwich as appropriate, using colored threads to accentuate the applied items and to add further detail as necessary.

TO MAKE ITEMS TO APPLY

Small precious items can be modeled out of colored craft modeling compounds, readily available in toy shops and from doll's house suppliers. Use cake decorator's cutters to create intricate shapes and prepare them with holes so that they can easily be attached to the quilt. The pieces should be fired in a domestic oven according to the manufacturer's instructions. I have used one of these compounds for buttons and found that it stands up satisfactorily to a wash in a washing machine. The advantage of such compounds is that a wide range of colors is available, although you need only buy a small selection as you can intermix them to create the exact colors you require.

STENCILLED QUILT

TO PLAN AND DESIGN YOUR QUILT

For this technique it is difficult to work at a very small scale, so I suggest you use a piece of stencil card no smaller than 2 in square. Start by drawing a 2 in grid with perhaps a border to fit the chosen size of quilt. The quilt illustrated, with twelve squares and a small border, measures 6½ x 8½ in and is based on a pot of flowers. Draw simple colored shapes into the squares, possibly using a traditional idea seen on an American 19th-century quilt or basing the pattern on a popular appliqué design. I've suggested some suitable designs in Fig. 21. It is best to use a white or pale fabric for the background. More detail, such as the stems of flowers, can be added to the quilt during quilting or with fine embroidery.

MATERIALS NEEDED

pencil and ruler

white paper

masking tape

thin card or stencil card

craft knife and cutting board or equivalent

oil sticks (e.g. Markal Paintstiks)

old plate for palette

small stencil brush

sewing thread and tools

cotton fabric

interlining if required

cocktail stick

TO MAKE THE STENCIL

Choose your design and draw it onto a piece of stencil card 2 in square. Working at this scale, any thin card – such as a postcard – will do for a stencil. Adapt your design so that the shapes remain isolated. Make sure you do not run one shape into another or the stencil will fall apart when cut. Cut out the design, using a board and a sharp craft knife. I find that the disposable craft knives are best for miniature work because they are lightweight and therefore less clumsy to use.

TO PREPARE TO STENCIL

Draw a 2 x 2 in heavy lined square grid the size of the quilt onto paper. Fix the paper to your work surface with masking tape. Place the quilt fabric over this grid and secure it with tape. The grid should show through the fabric.

Fig. 21
Stencil ideas

TO STENCIL

Place the stencil onto the first square and hold it in place with a small piece of masking tape. Choosing oil sticks that match your color scheme, place blobs of paint onto a plate. The paint should then remain moist as you work. Pick up some color with a stencil brush and lightly brush the color with a circular movement into the holes of the stencil. Print one color at a time, moving the stencil from square to square. Next, mask the first holes and print with a second color, then a third and so on until the stenciling is complete and all the squares are filled. Keep everything clean by masking the edges of the stencil with a piece of paper as you work. Take care to avoid any thick lumps of paint. The stencil brush can be cleaned between colors with washing-up liquid poured into the palm of your hand. Small details can be added with the tip of a cocktail stick and parts of the stencil can be used to print borders by masking off any holes that are unwanted. Leave the stencil print to dry for at least an hour. Excess color can then be ironed off onto clean absorbent paper; the ironing will also make the color permanent.

TO MAKE THE QUILT

Make the quilt sandwich and prepare the edge as appropriate. Quilt where desired with colored thread to enhance the design and to add detail. Finish the edge to complete the quilt.

VARIATIONS

There is no limit to the variations on stencil design that can be made, and the grid can also be based on a shape other than a square. So, together with the freedom of space and color, there are no limits – just your courage. I prefer traditional oil sticks for stenciling, but there is no reason why any of the numerous fabric paints and markers available in craft shops should not be used. Be sure that the paints you use are not too runny and that you lightly load your brush. Follow the manufacturer's instructions for fixing the colors.

SASHIKO QUILT

TO PLAN AND DESIGN YOUR QUILT

First decide on the size of your quilt. It could measure 7½ x 10 in and be made like a traditional Japanese quilt with white lines on a navy background. Draw an outline of the quilt to size and within this draw straight lines to divide it into a collection of simple geometric shapes. Into these, draw geometric patterns such as those illustrated in Fig. 22 to complete your plan. The design is now ready to be transferred to the quilt top. The quilt illustrated has a basic layout of squares which are filled with traditional Japanese patterns.

MATERIALS NEEDED

    fine plain navy cotton for the top and
        back of the quilt
    white sewing thread
    sewing tools
    white pencil
    masking tape

TO PREPARE AND MAKE THE QUILT SANDWICH

Fix the quilt top to your work surface with masking tape and draw the quilt design onto the fabric with a white pencil. Cut out a backing fabric and make the quilt sandwich. Prepare the edge as appropriate.

TO MAKE THE QUILT

Quilt the design in white thread, following the marked patterns. Work in a systematic way, up one row and down the next within each section until a whole pattern is quilted. Finish with a row of quilting round the edge and remove the tacking to complete the quilt.

VARIATIONS

The quilt layout could be divided with simple curved or wavy lines instead of the straight ones illustrated to give a softer look to the geometric patterns. Any strong contrast in tone or color between the fabric and the quilting thread would make a pleasing result.

EASY METHOD

There are a number of printed geometric-patterned fabrics that could be quilted, or simple geometric patterns could be quilted into the squares of a large-check or gingham fabric.

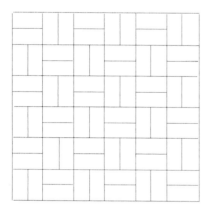
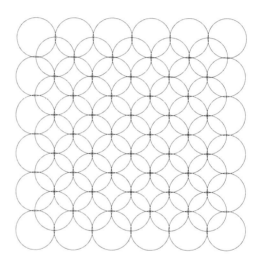

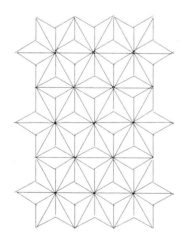
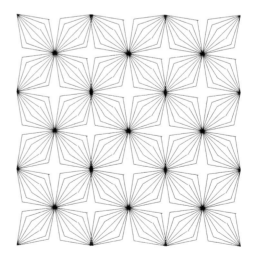

Fig. 22
Sashiko patterns

Chapter 3
The Quilt on Show

The quilts that you make have many different potential uses. They can be displayed in a doll's house, played with in a child's doll's house, framed or used as a small wall hanging. In this section I give the instructions for making a $\frac{1}{12}$th-scale miniature brass bed, a pine bed, a cot, a mattress, a pillow, blankets and bed linen for use with the quilts in a doll's house. Also provided are instructions for a

$\frac{1}{12}$th-scale quilt stand, based on the design of the full-sized version used by my own quilting group for displaying their quilts. This can be used in a doll's house or placed on the mantelpiece in your living room for all to see. I have ended with the suggestion that the quilts should be labeled for posterity and have provided suggestions on how to store them and ensure they are kept in prime condition.

DOUBLE BRASS BED

MATERIALS NEEDED

brass strips:

a 4 (¼ x 0.032 x 4¾ in) for head and footboards

b 4 (¼ x 0.032 x 4¾ in) for head and footboards

c 4 (¼ x 0.064 x ⅝ in) for brackets

brass tubes:

d 2 (⁵⁄₃₂ x 3 in) for inner legs

e 2 (⁵⁄₃₂ x 3¾ in) for inner legs

f 4 (³⁄₁₆ x 1 in) for spacing

g 8 (³⁄₁₆ x ½ in) for spacing

h 2 (³⁄₁₆ x ¾ in) for spacing

j 2 (³⁄₁₆ x 1½ in) for spacing

k 4 (³⁄₁₆ x ³⁄₁₆ in) for spacing

l 8 (³⁄₃₂ x 1⅞ in) for footboard bars

m 8 (³⁄₃₂ x 2⅝ in) for headboard bars

rectangular brass rods:

n 2 (³⁄₁₆ x ³⁄₃₂ x 6½ in) for side rails

wood for frame:

o 2 (¼ x ¹⁄₁₆ x 6¼ in) for rectangular frame

p 2 (¼ x ¹⁄₁₆ x 4¼ in) for rectangular frame

q 4 (⅛ x ⅛ x 6¼ in) for sides and support to fit bedstead

r 9 (¹⁄₁₆ x ½ x 4½ in) for slats

s 4 small pieces of soft wood to fill leg ends

4 brass knobs

4 castors

metal glue and wood glue

tools:

hacksaw

razor saw

needle file

mounted electric drill

vice for round tubing

set square

METHOD OF CONSTRUCTION

Drill holes to fit tubing in brass strips a and b as indicated in Fig. 24. Cut slots by drilling holes in the inner tubes d and e 2.5 cm (1 in) from the end to fit bracket c. File to ensure a firm fit. Glue c brackets in place, using a set square to check the angle. Cut slots in the bottom spacers f to fit round the bracket. Glue the bottom spacers in place on the inner tubes. Assemble the headboard and footboard using pieces g, h, j, k, l and m as indicated in Fig. 23 without glue first to check the fit. File holes as necessary. When you are happy with the fit, reassemble and glue. Fill the ends of the bed legs with a piece of soft wood s. Glue in place. Drill holes in the centre of the pieces of wood s to take the castors and the knobs, then glue these and the knobs in place to complete the head and footboards. Join the two bed ends with the side rails n fitting onto the brackets c. These joints may need to be filed to remove any burr from the sawing and glued if not a firm fit.

Make the wooden mattress frame by gluing **o** and **p** into a rectangle to fit the bedstead. Glue two of the pieces **q** onto the top, flush with the long edge. Fit and glue the nine pieces **r** across the frame, evenly spaced between the two pieces **q**. Glue the other two pieces **q** onto the bottom of the frame on the inside of the rectangle. These fit inside the bedstead and hold the mattress frame firmly in place. Sand and finish with oil or varnish as necessary.

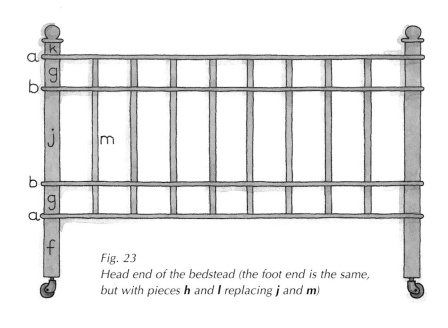

Fig. 23
Head end of the bedstead (the foot end is the same,
*but with pieces **h** and **l** replacing **j** and **m**)*

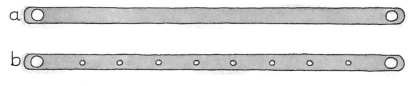

Fig. 24
Brass strips for head and foot ends

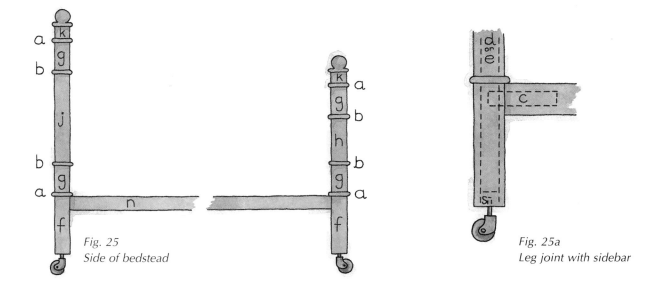

Fig. 25
Side of bedstead

Fig. 25a
Leg joint with sidebar

CRADLE

MATERIALS NEEDED

wood:

a   ³⁄₃₂ x 1½ x 2¾ in for base

b   2 (³⁄₃₂ x 1 x 2¾ in) for sides

c   ³⁄₃₂ x 1¼ x 11¹⁄₁₆ in for headboard

d   ³⁄₃₂ in x 1½ in x 11¹⁄₁₆ in for footboard

e   2 (³⁄₃₂ x ⅜ x 11¹⁄₁₆ in) for rockers

wood glue

fine-grade sandpaper

saw and craft knife

varnish or paint

METHOD OF CONSTRUCTION

Glue the two pieces b to either side of a, keeping the angle square. Glue c and d to the other sides of a to make the box shape of the cradle. Shape pieces e by rubbing with sandpaper or cutting them at an angle and rounding off the ends with sandpaper. These are the rockers for the cradle and need to be glued on the base of the box ¼ in from either end. Check that the cradle will rock evenly and sand if necessary. Wooden knobs may be stuck on the corners of the ends – I used an odd piece of cut-down doll's house stair rail for this. To complete the cradle, sand and then finish the wood with paint, varnish or Danish oil as desired.

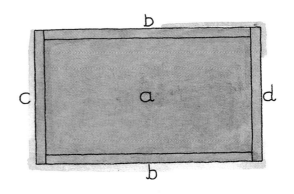

Fig. 26a
Base of cradle

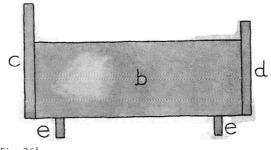

Fig. 26b
Side of cradle

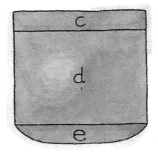

Fig. 26c
End of cradle

COT

MATERIALS NEEDED

wood:

a 4 (⅛ x ⅛ x 2 in) for legs

b 4 (⅛ x ⅛ x 4 in) for side bars

c 44 (1¾ x ⅛ in) dowels for cot rails

d 4 (⅛ x ⅛ x 3 in) for end bars

e 1 (1/16 x 2¼ x 4¼ in) for mattress base

wood glue

fine-grade sandpaper

saw and craft knife

varnish or paint

METHOD OF CONSTRUCTION

Make the ends of the cot by gluing seven evenly spaced dowels c between two pieces a, making sure that all is square. Make the sides in the same way, but with fifteen dowels c and two pieces b. Glue legs d to either end of the sides. Make the frame of the cot by gluing the ends to the sides, making sure all is square. Cut a ⅛ in square from each corner of piece e. Fit this, sanding if necessary, as the base to the cot. Glue in place. To complete the cot, sand and finish the wood with paint, varnish or Danish oil.

Decorative struts can be created by using ready-made rails for doll's house staircases instead of plain dowels. The ends of the cot can also be made with decorated flat pieces of wood.

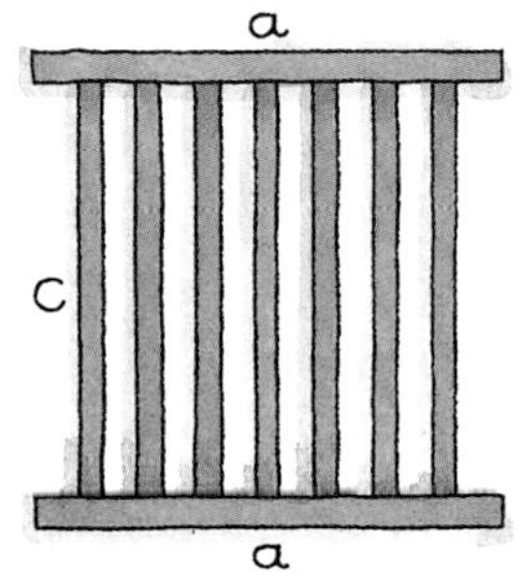

Fig. 27
End of cot

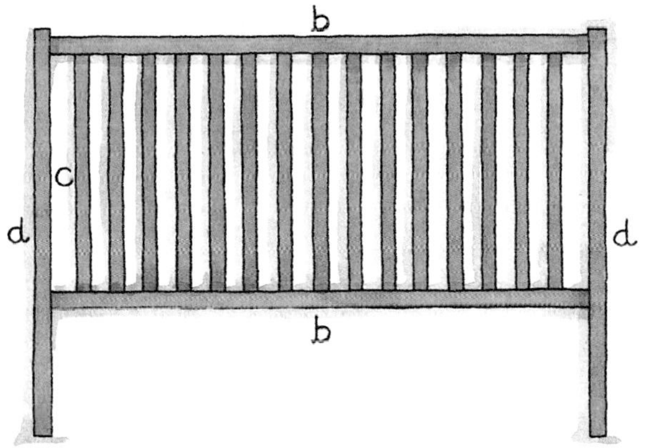

Fig. 28
Side of cot plus legs

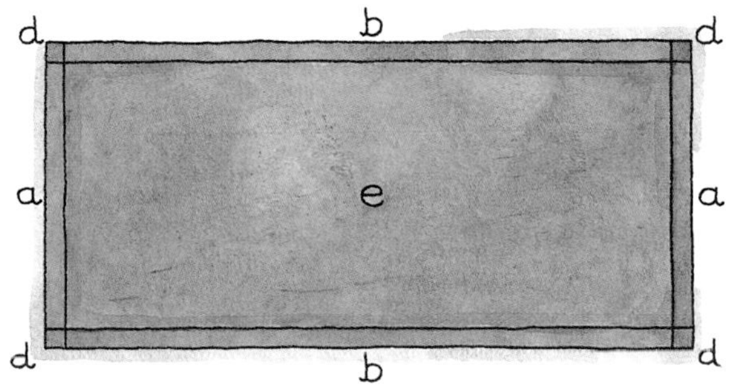

Fig. 29
Base of cot

SINGLE PINE BED

MATERIALS NEEDED

wood:

  a 2 (¼ x ⅛ x 6¼ in) for side bars of the mattress
     frame

  b 2 (⅛ x ⅛ x 6¼ in) for side bars of the mattress
     frame

  c 2 (¹⁄₁₆ x ⅜ x 2¾ in) for end slats of the mattress
     frame

  d 11 (¹⁄₁₆ x ¼ x 2¾ in) for slats of the mattress
     frame

  e 2 (¼ x ¼ x 3¾ in) for legs

  f 2 (¼ x ¼ x 3 in) for legs

  g 1 (⅛ x 2¾ x 2½ in) for headboard

  h 1 (⅛ x 2 x 2½ in) for footboard

wood glue

fine-grade sandpaper

saw and craft knife

varnish or paint

METHOD OF CONSTRUCTION

Glue a to b to make two L-shaped sections to hold
the side rails of the mattress frame. Cut a ⅛ in square
from two corners of both of the c pieces. Rest these
pieces on ab as shown in Fig. 32 to make the
rectangle of the mattress frame, with the extra ⅛ in
protruding. Stick in place. Space the pieces d evenly
between the side rails and glue down to complete the
mattress frame. Shape one end of each of the legs e
and f by rubbing them at angle with sandpaper or by
cutting a small groove round them ¼ in from the end
and rounding the end off with sandpaper. Shape the
tops of the headboard g and footboard h with a saw
and craft knife and sand to a smooth finish. Stick the

headboard flush with the edge of the legs e 1 in from
the bottom, and the footboard to legs f in the same
way. Finally, stick the mattress base to the head and
footboards with the ⅛ in protrusion fitting neatly
under them, making sure it is all square. Sand and
then complete the bed by varnishing or painting.

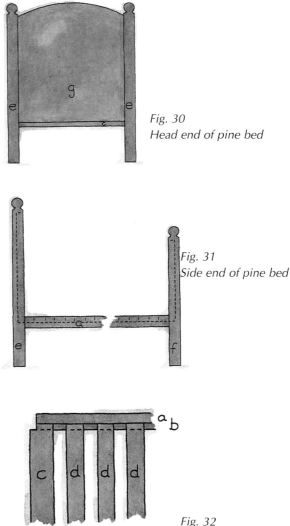

Fig. 30
Head end of pine bed

Fig. 31
Side end of pine bed

Fig. 32
Corner of mattress frame

Single pine bed with mattress and pillow

*Pine bed showing a
different style of foot and headboard*

used Danish oil to obtain a good pine appearance, but there are some very good, subtle-coloured paints on sale in DIY stores that make an attractive finish to wood.

A double pine bed can be made by adapting the necessary measurements. The head and footboards can also be redesigned and made up from a series of wooden strips instead of one flat piece – seen in the double pine bed illustrated above.

MATTRESS AND PILLOWS

MATERIALS NEEDED

striped cotton fabric to cover mattress:

a 2 [width of bed + ½ in x length of bed + ½ in]

b strip 1 in x length round the mattress + ½ in

striped cotton fabric for pillow:

c 3½ x 4½ in

small buttons or scraps of leather

layers of felt width of bed x length of bed

filling for pillow

sewing thread and tools

TO MAKE THE MATTRESS

Make a pile of the felt pieces to the depth of the
mattress and tack them together round the edge.
Next, make a bag for the felt mattress. Sew one side
of strip b all round the edge of one piece of a, and
the other side of the strip b round three sides of the
other piece of a. Turn the seams to the inside, stuff
the layers of felt into the bag and sew up the final
side of the bag. To complete the mattress, knot the
layers of felt and its cover together with small
buttons, or with small pieces of leather as seen on
an old style of mattress.

TO MAKE THE PILLOWS

Make a bag of the piece of cotton c by folding it in
half and sewing two sides together, turning the
seams to the inside. Stuff with just enough filling to
make the pillow feel soft. Sew up the last seam.

Fine-striped shirt cottons are eminently
suitable for covering mattresses and pillows, giving
the suggestion of ticking but not being too strong
in colour. The mattress interlining can be made
from any firm fabric such as layers of old blanket,
or, for a soft featherbed appearance, it could be
filled with kapok wadding.

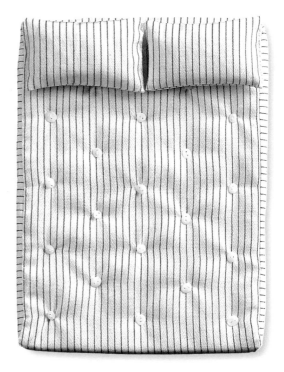

BLANKETS AND BED LINEN

Blankets can be made using a variety of different materials and techniques. For example, plain knitting makes a satisfactory covering. Using the finest needles you can find and a fine yarn, knit rows of garter stitch until the knitting measures 7½ in square. Darn in the ends of yarn and press. A miniature cellular blanket can be created by using different stitch patterns, and the edges of the blanket can be bound with a narrow, shiny ribbon. Crochet can give the look of an open-weave blanket. Two-ply yarn is the thinnest knitting yarn generally available, but a woollen crewel embroidery thread would produce a blanket that is considerably thinner. Doll's house suppliers sometimes keep a range of very fine needles for knitting.

Another way to make thin blankets is to use finely woven fabric and to paint the edges with a small amount of glue to stop them from fraying. I draw a rectangle of the required size onto the fabric and paint the glue on before I cut the shape out. There are glues on the market especially designed to stop cut edges fraying. For an underblanket I simply tear a piece of fine woolen fabric the same size as the mattress.

Sheets can be made from well-laundered and soft cotton fabric cut to fit the size of the bed plus allowances for tucking. The edges can be hemmed. Lace or trimming can be sewn to the top end to make the sheets very special. Instead of hemming, the edges can be painted with a glue to stop fraying. Pillowcases are made by cutting fabric slightly wider than and twice as long as the pillow, plus generous turnings at either end. Hem both narrow ends and turn one end over by ½ in. Fold in half and sew the seams on the two long sides, then turn it inside-out to complete a traditional pillowcase. The pillowcases can be decorated with lace or embroidery before the side seams are sewn.

QUILT STAND

MATERIALS NEEDED

wood:

a   2 (¼ x ¼ x 8½ in) for uprights

b   8 (⅛ x ½ x ⅞ in) for feet

c   1 (⅛ x 7 in) dowel for hanging the quilt

wood glue

fine-grade sandpaper

saw and ⅛ in drill

varnish

METHOD OF CONSTRUCTION

Saw off one corner of each piece b to leave a ⅜ in edge. Drill a ⅛ in-diameter hole through one end of each of the upright pieces a. Glue the feet pieces b round the other ends of the uprights (see Fig. 35), making sure each upright will stand securely. Sand and varnish. The dowel c is placed horizontally into the drilled holes; it is from this that your quilt will hang. For extra stability, second holes may be drilled at an equal distance from the base of each upright and a second dowel inserted. This dowel will also help the quilt to hang straight.

Before hanging a quilt, a narrow tube of fabric will need to be sewn onto the back of the quilt at the top as a sleeve through which the top dowel will fit.

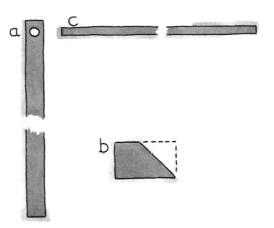

Fig. 33
Upright, dowel and base piece of stand

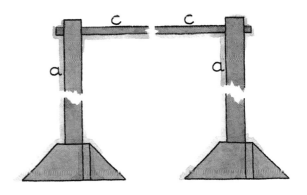

Fig. 34
Construction of main pieces

Fig. 35
Plan of quilt stand foot

THE DOLL'S HOUSE

The miniature quilts in this book will enhance any doll's house, whatever kind it is. You may have been lucky enough to inherit an antique doll's house or you might be refurbishing one for the next generation to play with and enjoy. Even a simple house made from a wooden or cardboard box can inspire the imagination, especially when filled with furnishings and a selection of miniature quilts.

Of course, it is possible to buy ready-made houses as well as those in kit form to build, decorate and furnish. But it can be fun creating a house from scratch. There are books giving instructions on how to do this and how to create different interiors (see page 110).

My doll's house, illustrated in this book, was made on a summer holiday several years ago by my husband from some basic drawings that I had made of our Victorian house. I have displayed quilts on the nursery walls and my work room, and on the beds, cot and cradle. Instructions for making beds, bed linen and a quilt stand can be found on pages 93-104.

CARE OF THE QUILTS

STORING YOUR QUILTS

When not in use, the miniature quilt should be stored carefully away from excess heat and damp, and out of sunlight. These will all make the fabric and thread of the quilt deteriorate over a period of time. A foil-lined cardboard box is a suitable container, the quilts stored inside between layers of acid-free tissue paper or layers of washed fabric to keep them free from dust, moisture and extreme temperature. If the quilts are displayed in a doll's house, do not keep them in place with pins but instead tack them in place with a needle and lightweight thread. Also, avoid leaving quilts tightly folded for any length of time, as in a miniature cupboard: creases are hard to remove and it would be a shame to spoil all the hard work put into making a beautiful quilt. Perhaps the best solution would be to change your miniature quilts as you would with full-size quilts during the normal run of household duties. Of course, a miniature quilt can be laundered if care is taken and no unusual materials have been used in its construction. Wash it gently by hand with a mild detergent in lukewarm water, rinse well and then dry flat. If any quilt should not be washed, then mark it clearly with a label stating this fact.

NAMING YOUR QUILTS

Why not name your quilts? If, like many of my quilts, they are to be used in connection with a family doll's house, then the chances are that they will outlive you, and I am sure the next generation would like to know who made them, when they were made and what inspired you to make them. So think about putting some indication of this information on the quilt, either with embroidery or a fine laundry pen. You might also like to keep a scrapbook with photographs and notes detailing how you made each quilt. Aside from providing a record, such a book would allow you to look back on memories. I have put a notebook beside my doll's house, in which I intend to add some of my miniature quilt designs, ideas and photographs, and perhaps some of the samples that did not quite make it to the final stages.

FURTHER READING

Jinny Beyer
The Quilter's Album of Blocks and Borders
Bell & Hyman (1982)

Valerie Campbell-Harding
Fabric Painting for Embroidery
B.T. Batsford (1991)

Averil Colby
Patchwork
B.T. Batsford (1987)

Sheila Smith and Freda Walker
Feltmaking – The Whys and Wherefores
Dalefelt Publications

Jill Kennedy and Jane Varrell
Silk Painting: New ideas and textures
B.T. Batsford (1995)

Carol and Nigel Lodder
Making Doll's House Interiors
David & Charles (1991)

Michal Morse
Build a Doll's House
B.T. Batsford (1992)

Linda Seward
*The Complete Book of Patchwork,
Quilting and Appliqué*
Mitchell Beazley

Dinah Travis
The Appliqué Quilt
B.T. Batsford (1993)

Dinah Travis
The Sampler Quilt Workbook
B.T. Batsford (1990)

Design tools and materials can be found at any
local art shop, and tools and materials for the beds
can be found at model shops.

INDEX

A
appliqué 23
  reverse 68
  quilt 65

B
beds
  double brass 94
  single pine 100
blankets and bed linen 103
block quilt 38
  designs 39
  layouts 40
  tree blocks 38
  patchwork 13
blocks 13
Bondaweb 23

C
care of quilts 109
cathedral window quilt 76
cot 98
cradle 97
crazy quilt 27, 57
  layouts 58

D
designing the quilt 10, 13
doll's house 106
drawing tools 10

E
embellished quilt 84

F
fabrics 16
  cotton 16
  prints 18
  recycled 16
  sateen 16
  sheer 48
felt quilt 66
frayed quilt 82

H
Hawaiian quilt 27, 47
  making a one-piece cut 47
  variations of design 49
hexagon quilt 28
  layouts 31

I
idea, recording first 10
interlinings 18

K
Kantha quilt 50
knots 24
knotted quilt 27, 78

L
log cabin quilt 27, 34
  layouts 37

M
materials 9, 16
mattress 102
Mola quilt 68

N
naming the quilts 109
needles 20

P
painted quilt 32
paints 10
paper quilt 27, 80
paper 10, 13
patchwork 21
  onto a backing 22
  over papers 21
  without papers 22
pillows 102
planning the quilt 10
printed quilt 60

Q
quilt
  construction 25
  edges 25
  on show 93
  sizes 12
  stand 104
quilting 24
quiltmaking techniques, basic 21

R
repeated block patterns 40
Roman stripes quilt 44
  layouts 46

S
Sashiko quilt 89
  patterns 90
sashing 13
sewing machine 18
silk painting 32
Somerset star quilt 54
  apply the patches 56
squares, quilt of 27, 70
  layouts 72
  variations of design 72
stencil design 88
stencilled quilt 86
stitches
  blanket, buttonhole,
    hemming, herringbone,
    machine zig-zag 23
storing the quilts 109
Suffolk puff quilt 42
  arrangements 43

T
techniques, basic 9
templates 13, 20
threads 18
tools 16
treeblock quilt 41
tucked quilt 73
  layouts 75

W
wadding 18
webbing, fusible 23
wholecloth quilt 52
  traditional patterns 52
workplace 20